Making *Love* with *Love*

How to Better Understand Us

Leonnardo Andre, MD.

The Reading Glass Books
1-888-420-3050
www.readingglassbooks.com
production@readingglassbooks.com

Dedicated to my wife, who showed me that the content of this book is not a utopia but an achievable endeavor.

Table of Contents

Introduction

The purpose of this book is to help bring couples closer to each other.
This book is to be used as an instrument for the growth for couples in their better understanding of their sexual intimacy by:

1. Identifying the wrong information that the person may have received in their upbringing, that led them to think that sex is "Dirty", "Forbidden", or "Something to keep hidden". Therefore, by doing so, we can get over this misconception.
2. Understanding the true value of sexuality in the human being.
3. Improving or developing effective communication skills for the couple.
4. Opening the doors that can lead to a more intimate knowledge of your mate.
5. Discovering each other, so you can, openly share your emotions, your feelings, and even to trust your body to your partner.

6. An invitation to get rid of the inhibitions, and to liberate yourself of the chains of sexual repression so you can give yourself fully, with love, to your partner.
7. Read about opinions, from men and women about their likes, dislikes, cravings, experiences, and fears regarding sexuality.
8. Review important aspects about anatomy and physiology of sex, sexual health, contraceptive methods, and sexual diseases.
9. Make mention of how the use of accessories such as "adult videos", "sex toys", and others that could be introduced in the relationship of the couple.

I reiterate that the purpose is: ***"To make of this book an instrument to develop closeness, to promote growth, and to acquire a better understanding within the couple"***.

Information that can help to give the fire, the strength, and the passion to your relationship. Information that may allow you to surrender openly your emotions, feelings, and desires towards your partner.

The knowledge that you can get with this book may get you closer to that wonderful experience of... **"MAKING LOVE WITH LOVE"**.

What is the importance of sex for the Couple?

One of the pillars that holds our society is the union of the family, consequently, we could say the stability of the relationship in the couple is, indeed, one of the pillars that holds our society.

Unfortunately, today more than 50% of marriages end up in divorce. One of the main causes of divorce is the lack of understanding and bonding of the couple. Infidelity has as one of its main causes the dissatisfaction in the sexual intimacy.

Master & Jonson in their studies on Sexuality came to establish that:

*"IF THE SEXUAL CONTACT BETWEEN
PARTNERS IS UNSATISFACTORY, THE
UNION OF LOVE CAN BREAK, AND
THE COUPLE WILL SEPARATE, EITHER
PHYSICALLY OR EMOTIONALLY"*

Although "good sex" in the couple is not the answer for happiness of the marriage, it is most definitely, especially important.

Humans can relate to other humans in different ways by being friends, neighbors, colleagues, relatives, coworkers, classmates, etc. In all these relationships there can be positive feelings, including love, but <u>the "relationship with a spouse" is different from all because with the spouse, is with whom the sexual intimacy is shared.</u>

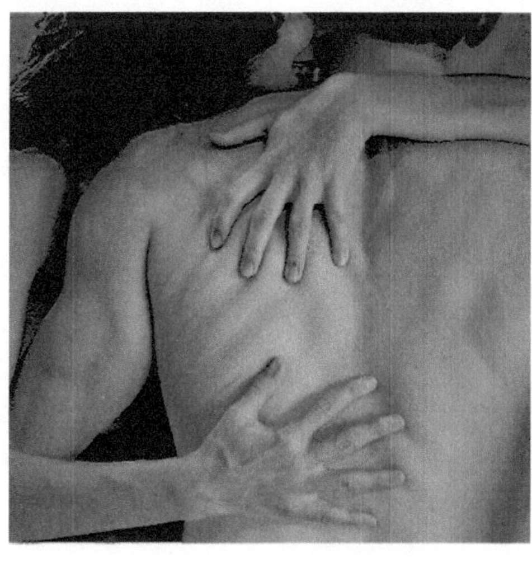

The presence of physical affection and sexual intimacy has been shown to be a strong predictor of satisfaction, affection, and likability in the relationship. During sexual intimacy Oxytocin is produced and, this hormone promotes bonding, reduces stress and, boosts trust in the marriage.

When marriage is lacking this important intimate element (sex), it can lead to feel unimportant, underappreciated, and self-conscious.

Therefore, it is obvious to say that sex is particularly important in the life of a couple.

If you love your partner, if you want to preserve or strengthen the union with him/her, if your partner is valuable to you, then proceed to give yourself permission to fully enjoy each other in the intimacy.

Take an active role and show openly your partner that you love him/her. Enjoy sexuality together to the fullest, enjoy that great bliss that "making love with love" brings.

Is it important to have knowledge about human Sexuality?

Some people may think that there are some things that are better left in the dark, in mystery, in ignorance. It may be so for other issues, but when it comes to human sexuality this does not seem to be a good idea.

"The World Health Organization affirms that ignorance about Human Sexuality is one of the most important causes of sexual problems".

Sexuality (capacity for sexual things) has such an intense force for the human being that it is believed that hiding this information, pretending that it does not exist, or ignoring it, may negatively affect the individual as well as the relationship.

Ignoring sexuality in the life of a person can cause anguish, unfounded fears, pain, distress, and many other negative feelings.

Embracing and exploring sexuality can bring many positive aspects to the relationship such as: euphoria, total release, relaxation, calmness, satisfaction, and closeness for the couple.

The applicable and plain-spoken information about sexual intimacy can bring multiple benefits including:

a. The fading of the anguish to the unknown,
b. Greater understanding, harmony, and happiness for the couple,
c. A better acceptance of yourself and your mate,
d. The rebirth of sexuality in the couple,
e. Decrease in the divorce rate.

Therefore, we must approach this issue naturally. We must understand that informing ourselves about the sexual aspect of the relationship is of most importance, both individually and for the couple.

Why is it important to do It?

You may have heard something like this before:

"My wife is a decent woman, she is the mother of my children, I better not even think about doing "that" with her… she may get offended, even if I mentioned that to her".

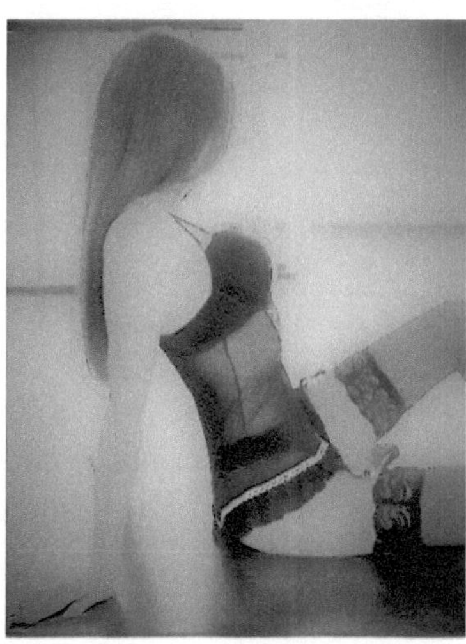

"On the other hand, with Francine (an imaginary name), I can do all those things, go wild, and satisfy my sexual cravings and desires."

Why is this a wrong concept? Why do so many times couples think that pleasure is only to be obtained outside the marriage?

To the contrary, the way it should happen is that, with your spouse, who is your friend, your partner, your lover, and your "accomplice"; precisely this is the person with whom all the sexual pleasures and delights should be procured.

With your spouse, you both should put all that passion and strength into enjoying the sexuality to the fullest.

It is time to break this wrong belief, let us welcome the pleasures that life has to offer, and live them with your loving mate.

*"**The quality of your relationship can determine the quality of your life.**"*

One of the most important factors that contribute to the person's happiness is the nature of his/her relationship. The relationship is how both parts relate to each other. The bonds of connections, that are established, give the couple a sense of well-being more than any other human experience.

Of course, it is not as easy as it sounds, because neither him nor her may not share the same point of view. There can be some disagreements, for example, it could happen that, for him or her, it may be "out of question" to consider making love in a different way as the partner may suggest.

One of the most common grounds for divorce lies in this misconception that, if a person wants to enjoy sex, he or she needs to look for it outside of the relationship. Unfortunately, due to diverse factors, many people think this way.

Let me remind you that what differentiates the spousal relationship with other types of human relationship is precisely the presence of sexual intimacy, trust, companionship, dependability, support, and love.

It would be outstanding if the couple would come to feel the following:

"Together we do all the sexual mischief, and delights than our imagination can conceive. We have such a wonderful time, and feel we are united, friends, lovers, and accomplices. We feel we give each-other this beautiful gift of life: Ourselves. Now we feel physically, emotionally and spiritually closer than ever."

"The Desire is Gone"

Pete and Lucy, after being together for about one and a half years, fell in love and decided to get married. Only after three years of married life everything became so different, what could have happened?

The frequency of love contacts had decreased dramatically as the years passed by. They both started to blame each other.

Now they spend their time doing everything but dedicating time to each other. Now they pass mostly worried about how to maintain a level of financial income to maintain a lifestyle to show for, they spend their time in issues with childcare, and other daily tasks.

Things changed to the point that seems they only cohabitate under the same roof. For them, sexual intercourse turned into nothing more than a burden, a way to attenuate a separation or a possible conflict. Sex as duty or obligation trying to cover up the crisis and its consequences.

At the beginning of their relationship, when they first got to know each other, they used to do everything on their part to conquer the other, to fall in love. In the past, both would put their time and energy into cultivating the bonds of intimacy.

After being married, they took for granted the need to continue conquering each other, the need to continue giving their loving attention.

It seems that this couple had been taken over by a silent and erroneous concept of feeling: "I don't have to make any efforts anymore… I already have you."

She complains that it seems he no longer cares about her, and that he only shows to her some affection so he can have sex.

On the other hand, He feels rejected since she shows no interest in intimacy. Both suffer and both feel they are the victims and the other one is to be blamed.

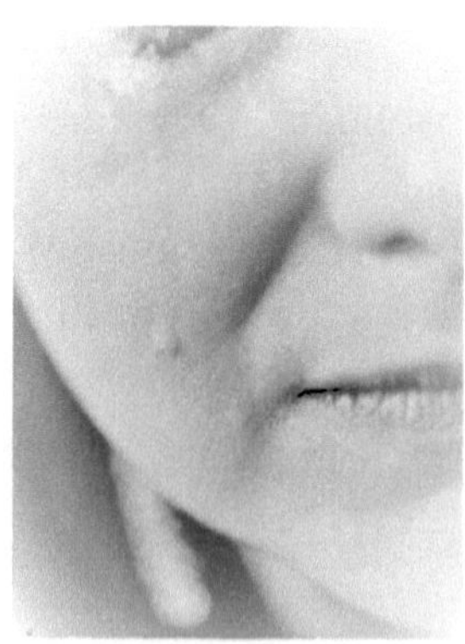

<u>As long as sexuality is not validated, not recognized, as a very important dimension in the human experience, people will have many limitations to understand their partners.</u>

"The lack of creativity, the lack of continuous emotional affectionate support, and the lack of fulfillment in their sex life, will likely lead the couple to develop a growing distance as time passes on".

Lack of intimate sexual life is not just limited to the lack of physical proximity; it goes much further than that. The couples might argue for any reason, but then, when they make love, they appease the bad feelings, it is a kind of positive rebirthing, it is like a ritual of forgiving each other.

Making love is much more than just sex, it is feeling accepted, understood, loved and desired by the person that is so special for you … your spouse.

Returning to the couple from our initial example:
She complains that he is angry most of the time. His lack of patience and his bad mood were like poison to her soul. He seemed to get easily annoyed, even by any little thing. Being with him, she says, is like walking between crystal glasses, watch out not to have a wrong move or else.

He comments that all she does is "complain all day and about everything", and that she always finds some fault in him. "It seems she is always looking for excuses for not being intimate with me" he says. It used to be enjoyable and fun to spend time with her.

Both have entered into this negative swirl of blaming each other.

By doing this, all they get is to sink further in despair and to distance themselves more from each other. Their concentration is more in trying to prove the other wrong than trying to seek solutions.

Curiously, this couple still wanted to be with each other. When he gave his side of the story he said: "Besides the fact that it is good for the kids, I still hope that we can rediscover the magic that one day brought us together". "She was my best friend and, I used to love her company" he said.

Unfortunately, there came a point where everything started to change and now we are so estranged and hurt.

On the other side, she says that after the birth of her first child, she felt exhausted, unable to sleep well, not even a single night. At times, she felt so tired that the last thing on her mind was having yet to take care of another subject.

As time went by, the countless times of rejection and disapproval of her towards him, had produced an increasing pain and anger in her husband. As a result, he progressively stopped putting his time and energy into the relationship.

This couple, with their incessant accusations of each other, their lack of mutual consideration, their coldness, their body-language, and verbal rejection had turned them into a couple without ties.

The bonding force that sexual intimacy can give was no longer present.

In the marriage, if the need for affection and sex is ignored, not given proper importance, belittled, or even ridiculed, the bonds of the couple will suffer and it is only a matter of time for distancing to occur, be it physical and/or emotional.

Sex is extremely important for the relationship in the couple. When sex is good and satisfying for both, this offers couples the opportunity to give and receive physical pleasure, in addition to connect emotionally and spiritually.

"Sex with love" builds closeness, intimacy, and a feeling of companionship.

This defines their relationship as different from all other human relationships. Simply put, "sex can be a powerful force that binds".

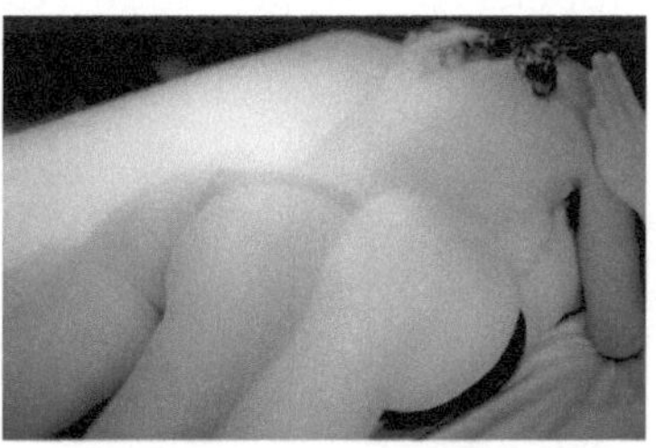

Our couple in question leads a parallel life, under the same roof, in the same bed, involved in similar activities of physical proximity, but without any emotional or physical connection.

Feelings of anger surface the skin, the friendship between them evaporates, the lack of understanding prevails, and the emotional divorce becomes unavoidable.

For someone like Pete, sex has great importance. "Sex with love" is much more than simple physical pleasure, it is connection, intimacy, closeness, and affection. For Pete it is about feeling attractive, masculine and feeling valued as a person. It is about feeling loved.

Since Lucy does not seem to have much interest in the sexual part of the relationship, as she does not feel that need, she has no sympathy for what happens to her partner and does nothing about it.

Eventually these feelings of rejection will become more difficult to handle, sadness may turn into anger.

Those who seek sexual intimacy and do not find it, they become resentful, angry, and distant.

Although this behavior is only a symptom of an injured person, this is not perceived like such by the partner and sympathy and compassion are scarce.

The fights over the subject of sex, or lack of it, have become the norm, disagreements proliferate and the only thing they do is blame to each other. Nothing seems to be good anymore.

Does the described story sound familiar to you?

Have you felt rejected, or overwhelmed in a similar relationship?

Do you feel that your physical and emotional issues are not been taken care of or considered?

Does it hurt the lack of interest in intimacy by your partner?

Do you feel frustrated and sad with so much fighting that never ends?

Thinking about divorce or separation?

Have you ever felt hopeless and as if there is no light at the end of the tunnel?

Have you reached the point of giving up?… If you have answered yes to any of these questions, then you know that your relationship is in danger.

The person with less interest in sexual intimacy may say: "But, if I do not have interest in sex, why should this be my problem?", therefore, "why am I to do anything about it?"

Although good sex is not a "sure ticket" to happiness in the marriage, it is, most definitely, a particularly important ingredient.

If you want to preserve your marriage and prefer to be happily married, you'd better start paying attention to this aspect of your relationship.

You need to know that once you start paying more attention to the emotional and physical aspect of the relationship and start again having loving sex with your partner, he (or she) will feel happier.

To be around happy people, unlike bitter people, is more bearable. When people are happy, they tend to become more considerate, more affectionate, more positive, and more communicative. This is human nature.

When you show your interest in your partner about what matters to him or her, "magic" will happen in the relationship.

By demonstrating to your partner that "you care", that things that are important to him/her are also important to you, he or she may notice it and, in turn, become more attentive to your needs. This change may spark the beginning of regaining the strength that the relationship had in the past.

When you become more involved in sexual intimacy with your spouse, even if initially your desire may not be totally into it, you may get to discover that, your sexual appetite had not disappeared but that it was only asleep.

It is common to see that a person who initially did not feel sexually aroused, after starting the caresses and sexual affection may feel stimulated and enjoy it.

Many sex counselors recommend that both, in the relationship, take the steps forward, taking an active role, even if initially the desire is not present.

Taking an active role does not only mean getting your mate undressed or verbalize your desire to go to bed. There may be subtle ways to show your participation and interest, like for the lady, to "casually" bend forward displaying her goods, to dress provocatively, to "casually" rub against his manhood; or for him to bring her flowers, tell her how pretty she looks, verbalize how appreciative he is of her care, send her a sweet text during the day, etc. It would also help not to just stay still during the intimacy.

If you do not experience sexual pleasure, or if you do not reach an orgasm, you may think that "having intercourse" with your spouse, makes no sense, but it is important to understand that the effects of sexual intimacy go far beyond the mere physical aspect, it can open doors to the emotional well-being for both.

When a person loves his or her partner, it usually makes them happy to please their spouse and make them smile.

Bringing passion back into your relationship is not an exact science, you have to proceed with the philosophy of "**<u>try and keep trying until you find what helps</u>**".

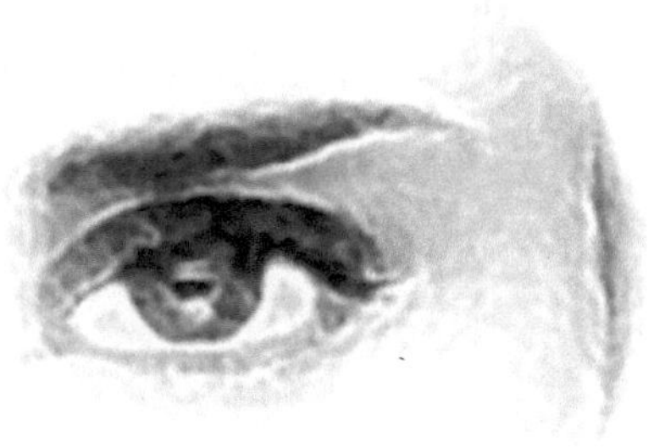

Although the concept of trying, even without having the desire, sounds not too romantic, the reality is that when the initial physical attraction is exhausted, which inevitably happens over time, sexual desire and sexual activity becomes a choice.

> *You can decide to have a sexual relationship that is vibrant, exciting, and satisfying as one of the most important priorities of your married life.*

You are encouraged to discover and rediscover new ways to keep your sexual energy alive. If you want to "get back" your relationship, you should deliberately and consciously do your part to keep reinventing what keeps vibrant and fulfilling your sexual relationship with your partner.

This will not happen by itself; you may need to take an active role and make it happen.

Perhaps you are ready to take your couple relationship in a more productive and positive path.

You may be wondering if a life that includes sexual satisfaction, is within your reach. Well, the answer is YES, but only, if you are willing put your interest and dedication in it.

Now I turn to the one in the couple who felt rejected. The fact that your partner did not show any interest in improving his/her sexual life with you may have made you feel frustrated, devastated, hurt, rejected, and abandoned.

But please do not rush in just accusing your partner. The responsibility that things are not going well lies in both of you. The problems usually occur when conflicting issues arise combined with the unproductive way people respond to them. (Lack of effective communication).

The feelings of pain, resulting from feeling rejected, will often lead to a defensive behavior, and this will not likely help to the solution of the problem.

Trying to have a less reactive attitude and to start with a more positive and understanding attitude may help.

You may wonder and how do I do it?

Well, let us start by trying to find the reason why the other one seems to be not interested.

Most of the time the root is going to be emotional. The lack of respect, consideration, recognition, patience, and understanding can distance a person.

Other possible causes could be trauma during their upbringing that may have caused a subconscious negative attitude towards their mate.

Could it also be physical due to some underlying illness? If the answer does not seem to be easily accessible it may require a visit to the medical doctor and to a sexual therapist.

Remember that focusing on the solution will get you further than only going around and around complaining about the problem.

VI

Working together in the Solution

The ideal scenario is that both in the couple are willing to participate in understanding the problem (emotional and/or physical distancing) and looking for a solution, but it is possible that only one of you has shown this interest.

Please do not feel helpless that there may be many things you can do. For a change to occur in the relationship one of you should take the initiative, and take the first step, it may be your turn now.

You can only control what you think and what you do. You are only responsible for your words and for your actions.

Try to first listen, afterwards you may have your saying to a more receptive person.

During a conversation, when you first listen and let the other one says what is in his/her mind, you may be at an advantage. First listening will often lead to the other one listening back to you. In addition, when you first listen, you get the knowledge to better understand what the other one is thinking and feeling.

Seek first to understand, then to be understood
—S. Covey

When you show actions of caring towards your mate, likely the other one will reciprocate. Instead of making a negative remark, try to say the same thing in a positive way. For example: "You don't cuddle with me anymore" (sounds like an accusation), you can say "I enjoy when we stay longer holding softly".

It may be necessary that one of you takes the initiative to improve the relationship, then the other one may follow. Ultimately it may help to understand that BOTH of you need to make changes.

Way too often, when couples experience difficulties in their sexuality, they suffer alone and in silence.

They avoid talking about the subject in an open and honest way because they may feel uncomfortable or ashamed.

To keep it quiet and for yourself is sad. Most people do not have the ability to read the mind of others, especially when it comes to sexual satisfaction.

It may be challenging to know exactly what both of you want or need. It would be most helpful for the couple to open the door of communication and share that information openly.

*Most of sexual problems in the couple are
due to the lack of effective communication
on issues that are delicate and personal.*

Part of what may need to be done will be to improve this communication, and to open the doors to start talking and touching again.

A team effort will likely give you the most favorable results, BOTH OF YOU MAY NEED TO BE MORE FLEXIBLE AND BETTER ADDAPT TO EACH OTHER NEEDS.

The couple can first decide, and accept that, ***a sexual life with love is of most importance***.

*Then they can give themselves permission
to explore sexuality in an open and honest
way to find the treasures that it keeps.*

*INSTEAD OF CONTINUE ARGUING ON THE
DIFFERENCES, AND WHO IS TO BLAME,
THE COUPLE SHOULD BECOME ALLIES
AND COMPANIONS IN LOVE, TO SEARCH
TOGETHER FOR THE SOLUTIONS.*

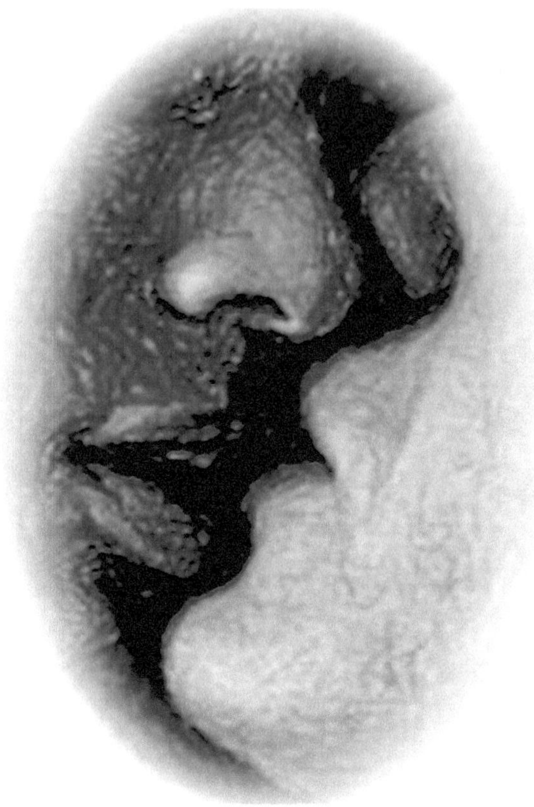

In a truthful manner, both of you, each separately, can make a list of five of the qualities you find in your partner and then share it with each other.

Nobody likes to be criticized and everyone likes to be valued. A sincere compliment goes a long way.

VII

"Not today, ...I have a Headache"

We will refer to the instance when "I have a headache" is just an excuse to avoid having sexual intercourse. Similar expressions include: "I'm tired", "I do not feel well", or without words to show indifference.

With great wisdom, it has been commented that:

*"When sex goes well in the couple, it contributes to
35% of the stability and happiness, but, when sexual
intimacy does not go well, it suddenly becomes 90%
of the reason for the unhappiness of the couple".*

*While "harmony in bed" is not everything, it sure
is very important for the wellbeing of the couple.*

*<u>Let us remember that when there is a breach in
the sexual understanding of the couple, this causes
a distancing, either physical and/or emotional.</u>*

*One of the most powerful sexual stimulants that exists is
knowing that your sexual partner strongly desires you.*

The feeling of being lusted by your mate, not just makes the person happy, it goes even further, invites, stimulates, and feeds the soul. The understanding of feeling desired by the partner makes the person feel accepted and loved.

To the contrary, when a person feels their mate does not want or desire him/her, it translates into "I don't love you today", "you don't have what it takes for me". It is the feeling of rejection that is the opposite of feeling loved and "Making love with love".

"Rejection destroys the bonding in the relationship."

When having sex has become a burden, when sexual intercourse has turned into something monotonous without positive emotions, having sex under these circumstances will likely make the person feel used.

Having sex as an obligation, just to fulfill your marital duties, without desire, without fire, without passion, without bonding, without affection makes you wonder if there is still love in the relationship.

Resentment, unresolved conflicts, betrayal, lack of respect can be a major turnoff in the relationship. Being in this situation can place the couple one step away from divorce.

One, or both, in the relationship, may be hurt by some incidents that may have occurred in the past. Try to investigate them and "focus on the solution, not on the problem". With a positive attitude, with patience, with control over your negative emotions, and above all, with lots of love, you can seek to resolve this situation that harms the union of the couple.

If this is what is happening to you in your relationship, please put your best effort and open the doors to dialogue. BOTH of you may need to give in and try to accommodate your partner's needs.

*<u>The emotional aspect is responsible of more than 50%
of the success in establishing "harmony in the bed".</u>*

***Only after the emotional aspect has been
attended properly, then there is a good
possibility of finding pleasure and complete
fulfillment in the couple's sexual life.***

The Lack of Sexual Desire

The causes for lack of sexual desire can be diverse. The more common causes are of psychological origin.

Between them we find:

- **<u>Stress and fatigue</u>:**

    This tends to be transient because, when the individual feels rested, sexual desire returns. It is important that the couple seek to routinely spend moments away from daily stress, that both try to carry out activities to relax and have fun together. Both should seek and plan time together and, alone as a couple, to give each other quality time, just as they did at the beginning of the relationship.

- **<u>Anxiety:</u>**

    This feeling is described by many as "The sensation of intense, excessive, and persistent worry and fear about everyday situations, the sensation that something bad is about to happen". Anxiety is an unpleasant feeling of imminent danger, yet many times not apparently related to any specific situation.

Human beings tend NOT to behave to its best when feeling very anxious. Anxiety goes hand in hand with fear.

A man with anxiety may have difficulty in getting an erection (erectile dysfunction), may suffer from premature ejaculation (having an orgasm too quick after starting sex), or simply a lack of sexual desire.

Likewise, the woman who suffers from anxiety, usually caused by fear, will also not be able to enjoy sexual intercourse.

The woman with anxiety may suffer from Anorgasmia (inability to reach an orgasm), Vaginismus (contraction of vaginal muscles that prevent penetration), etc.

- **<u>Suppressed anger:</u>**

  A person who is angry at his/her partner may express frustration through apathy and lack of sexual desire. It may be difficult to start the love game when there are unresolved conflict situations. Other times the underlying anger may be due to previous negative experiences with the opposite sex in the past. Even worse when the suppressed anger is not even related to the relationship but to other issues in life.

- **<u>Feelings of rejection</u>:**

  When a person perceives a lack of interest in his/her partner, or worse, a rejection of intimacy, this may eventually produce the development of a lack of sexual desire towards his/her partner.

- **<u>Other non-psychological causes</u>**:

  Although the psychological causes are the most common, likewise, there may be other causes such as: hormonal deficiencies, debilitating and chronic illnesses, pain of any cause, side effects to certain medications, etc.

To be able to experience pleasure, one needs to have a basic sense of self-worth which says: "I am loveable", a basic sense of self-esteem which says: "I am desirable" and then, the ability to communicate and share your wishes, likes and dislikes with your partner. Sexual desire is the art of wanting, maybe not wanting more, but mostly wanting better sex.

What can be done in case of loss of sexual desire?

If you noticed a decline of your sexual desire for your partner, try to analyze what could be the cause. Of the many causes mentioned, maybe one or more may apply to your case. Be honest with yourself and then try to find a solution, on your own, with the help of your partner, or if necessary, seeking professional help.

Remember that "Romance" may be necessary to bring the sexual desire. We tend to be excited by the unknown, about the idea of losing control and by allowing a surprising new experience to unfold. Creativity is essential to keep the fire in passion.

Sex in a committed relationship sometimes may need to be a premeditated action. You both may need to plan in finding a special time for the two to be alone with the openness to engage in passionate play.

Sex is not something you do, instead, it is a place you go. It is a place to connect, a place to be naughty, tender, playful, to feel young and beautiful, a place for power, a place for surrender, a place for all that comes to your mind with a creative imagination and with a willing partner.

You could come to the realization that you feel you want it, you owe it, you deserve it, it is a good thing that you are entitled to get and you want to share it with your mate.

Conversation, negotiation, complicity, playfulness, thirst for adventure, attraction for the "forbidden" together, with a problem-solving attitude, can definitely help.

Remember that it is useless to identify the possible cause of the lack of sexual desire when nothing is done to improve it. If you can find the cause, then focus on resolving these issues.

On the other hand, if you cannot identify the cause of lack of sexual interest towards your partner, if the two of you cannot work on resolving this issue by yourselves, then seek attention with your doctor and/or a Sexual therapist.

Beyond the External and Superficial Appearance

Many couples have one fight after another and, unfortunately, they only focus on observing what apparently caused that argument. Many times, a person is already irritable that, even the fly of an insect can set them off.

When a person feels dissatisfied, frustrated emotionally or sexually, he/she becomes irritable, upset, gets hostile, and everything seems to indicate, that, "there is no light at the end of the tunnel".

Many times, it is easier to explain a conflict based on a trivial act, than to engage in analyzing the <u>underlying problems</u>, even worse when the problem is sexual.

The very person, who is in the middle of the conflict, may not even recognize that as an example, what is bothering her is that it has been more than two months since she had an orgasm; or in his case, what actually annoys him is that she always rejects him or shows no interest in making love.

Many times, seems easier to blame the problem on a trivial act like one saying: "you are stupid" (when that was not the real problem), and the real problem could be the lack of respect.

It is possible that in the relationship neither of them can identify the real problem, and they limit themselves to only discussing the apparent problem, without solving the underlying real problem.

As a result, their relationship deteriorates and, in the end, the unavoidable happens… the physical and/or emotional breakdown.

If the real underlying problem is not identified and recognized there are very few possibilities of full understanding and resolving it.

Both should be honest, and talk about the conflict, at hand, that caused the quarrel, then ask yourselves if you were already upset by some other fact, even before the discussion. You may find that frequently that was the case.

For the couples that may have something similar happening to them, it may help them to try to identify the underlying problems that are affecting them.

With patience, respect, and love try to open a dialogue to seek the solution for you both.

"The attitude, and the conduct that you two gives to each other, can make all the difference".

Be sincere with each other and talk of the real problems, that "in the background", may be affecting you both.

Essential components for establishing good Communication

In a survey of hundreds of couples about sexuality, it was observed that a common factor that occurred in most of them, was the lack of effective communication.

Communication is the essential instrument for reaching a good understanding, better complementation, and thus, the happiness of the couple.

I want to reiterate the great importance of knowing <u>how</u> to communicate in human relationships, especially for the relationship in the couple.

If you place two people in a room, then tell them to proceed to agree on their differences, this may not lead to the resolution of their problems; to the contrary, the problems may get worse if, both, lack the ability of how to communicate.

Most of the necessary ingredients for good communication seem obvious, yet often they are not present when they are most needed, in the peak of a heated conversation.

The essential components to establish "efficient communication" are:

▶ **<u>KNOWING HOW TO LISTEN</u>**: Listening to the other person first is important and, knowing how to listen, can make all the difference. Listening, not only implies to be quiet while someone else talks, it goes beyond that, you must:
- Pay attention to what the other person is saying
- Without interrupting
- Without prejudging
- Without insulting
- Giving importance to what the other says and giving credit to what you are listening to.
- You should tell yourself that the other person who is talking might be correct about what he/she is saying and, you ought to take it into account

► <u>**AVOID physical and verbal HOSTILITY**</u>.
- Keep calm
- Do Not scream
- Do not offend (do not insult)
- Do not start hitting walls, or throw objects
- Do not push or hit your partner.

► <u>**DO NOT ASSUME THINGS**</u> and come to your own conclusions without first giving an opportunity to the other one to explain himself or herself.

► <u>**EXPRESS YOURSELF WITH CALM, CONSIDERATION AND RESPECT**</u>

► <u>**DO NOT FEEL YOU ARE THE OWNER OF THE TRUTH**</u> and consider the possibility that the other person may be correct.

► <u>**DO NOT always BLAME**</u> the other person and consider the possibility that you may be mistaken.

► <u>**DO NOT GET DEFENSIVE**</u> and in response you attack.

► <u>**AVOID REPROACHES**</u> Try NOT to talk to the other in way that expresses disapproval, criticism, or disappointment.

► __AVOID THE NEGATIVE SWIRL__ of repeating the same about the problem, again and again, just trying to blame the other instead of concentrating in finding the solution for it. "Focus on the solution, not on the problem".

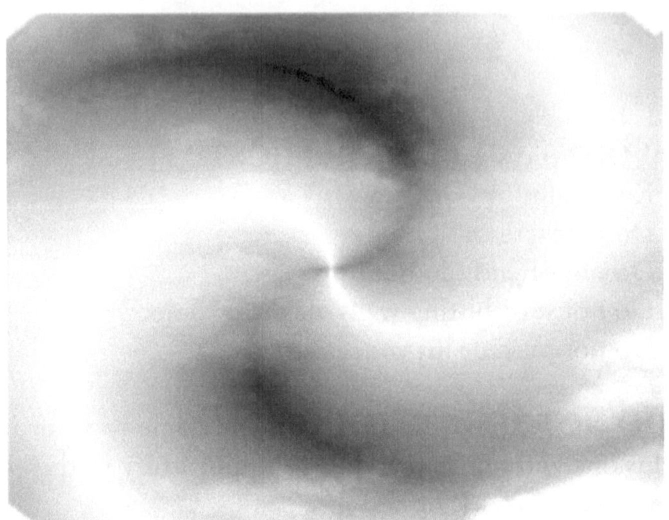

► __TAKE A POSITIVE ATTITUDE,__ avoid being pessimists, and on the contrary, believe that both of you CAN come to an understanding. **Focus more on the positive things you both have** and, above all, look for alternative solutions by giving positive suggestions.

▶ **<u>UNDERSTAND THAT A PATHWAY CAN BE BUILT WHILE WALKING</u>** "As you walk you leave a path". Just keep trying that you may find the way.

Every opportunity to establish a dialogue can be suddenly interrupted, when the points above described are not taken into consideration.

By improving your communication skills, for sure, both of you will win.

It is also important to procure an opportune and calm moment to establish communication, but on the other hand, do not postpone the dialogue indefinitely. <u>When there are problems, it is better to put a solution to them before they keep growing.</u>

However, from time to time, even with the best of intentions, it may be difficult to communicate without fighting or taking offense.

When the couple cannot establish a positive dialogue, it could be necessary to have the intervention of a neutral third person, like a counselor or a therapist to help them establish dialogue and open the doors to effective communication.

When trying to communicate with each other, please do not forget to consider the important points previously mentioned.

"It takes two to tango".

Both of you need to do your part to save or improve the harmony in the relationship.

The introduction of feelings, love and spirituality to the sexual intercourse will transform the experience. It will no longer be only "a delivery of the flesh", It will become a "manifestation of love", a beautiful work of growth, and approach between two beings who love each other.

What do we mean by "Making Love"?

Making love is not synonymous of intercourse (penetration of the penis into the vagina), this involves so much more.

Making love is the **full surrender of oneself** to the other with love. It is to allow yourself to do whatever your imagination permits, so that you can give and receive affection. In other words, you give yourself permission to give yourself completely.

Loving actions including flirting, romance, caresses, passion, sweet words, tender and sensual touching, loving attentions, with all the body and mind, with that force that comes from the deepest you… this is part of making love with love.

There are physical and psychological differences between a man and a woman. In general, women tend to be more sentimental and emotional; on the other hand, man tends to be more visual, physical, and practical.

In majority of cases, for <u>women</u>, sexuality is a projection of the emotional affection, <u>"first I feel all that emotional elation, then the desire to surrender my body"</u>.

On the other hand, for the man "the delivery of the body, full of passion and desire, fulfills him".

<u>For a man, when his wife shows passion and desire for him, he perceives as being loved.</u>

A man can get aroused more quickly than a woman.

After he ejaculates (has an orgasm), he will have a refractory period (inability of the penis to obtain an erection) that can prolong for minutes, hours or even days, depending on the age and health status of the individual; on the other hand, women can have one orgasm followed by another, with very short periods in between.

When a man ejaculates his level of sexual arousal drops precipitously, for the woman, on the other hand, she can have a steady level of enjoyment lasting much longer, the sexual stimulation can drop down more slowly.

Many times, "the gratification and pleasure will lie in giving pleasure and joy to your partner".

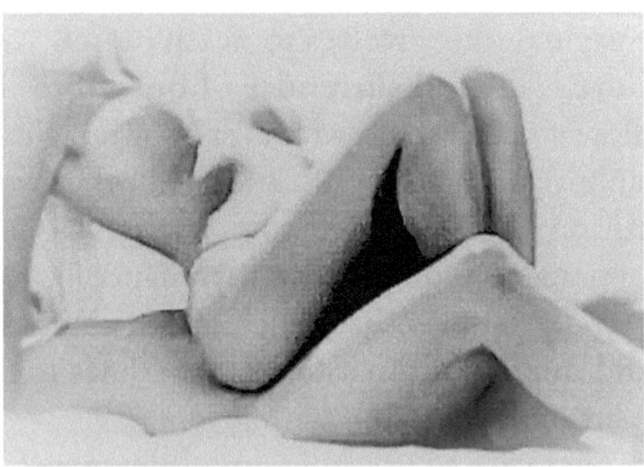

A serious mistake that many couples make is to take the attitude that the responsibility to feel pleasure is "in the hands of" the partner.

It is a mistake to think that the other person is the one who is "in charge" to give you pleasure.

Taking an attitude of totally being receptive and to think that reaching an orgasm will only happen if the partner stimulated appropriately, or if it did not happen was because the partner did not know how to do it, is a misconception.

To know how to sexually arouse and stimulate, with a good technique, your partner can definitively help but it is not all.

Reaching an orgasm is an individual responsibility. When, in love making, one seeks to please the partner, and the loved one is trying to do the same, this will increase the possibility of both experiencing pleasure. It is also important to focus on your own pleasure.

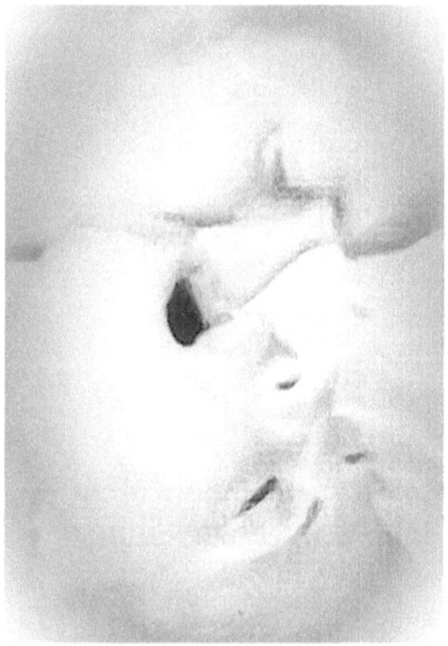

Reaching an orgasm is wonderful, but it is not the only means of satisfaction nor should be the only goal to be sought.

For example, when he has premature ejaculation, in few thrusts he reached an orgasm, and nobody really had much pleasure.

It has been said that, If Sex Had to Have a Goal,
It Should Be Pleasure—Not Orgasm.

Many times, you can help your partner on how to please you, by suggesting the things you like, similarly, be receptive and encourage your partner to do the same.

When "making love" stops having as the main ingredient love, then it becomes a mechanical act.

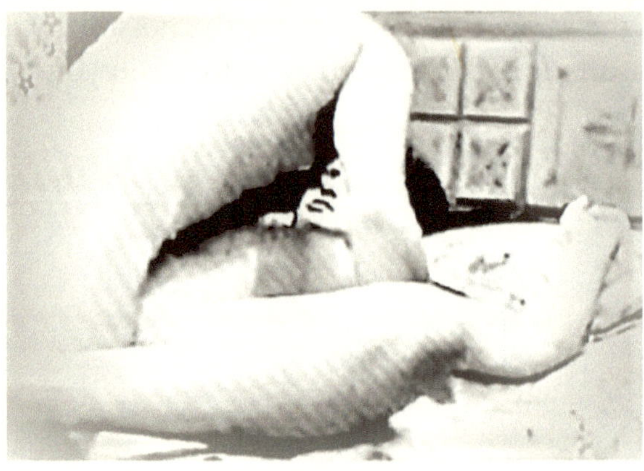

Under these circumstances, boredom problems, monotony, sex as duty, and the feeling of being used can arise.

We will likely fall short expressing in words the wonders of "making love with love".

For one person it may mean something different than for another, but one thing in common would be the presence of this grandiose feeling that touches us way deep inside.

"Love moves mountains", this intense feeling of deep affection has a strong power to transform lives. In marriage it can be said as: "Complete surrender of your being, mind and body, towards your mate".

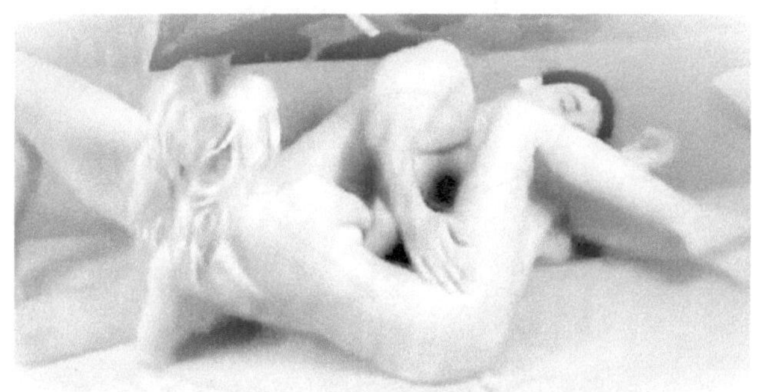

"My body vibrates, from the tip of my hair to the tip of my feet. Each and, every of my pores shed copious perspiration. My gasping breath blows to your ear murmurs of love. My surrender is complete and without reservations. My lips and my tongue insatiably explore your mouth and your whole body. My erect penis thrusting penetrates you once, then again and again. My heart beats with uncontrollable strength against your chest. In the middle of this sweet storm, like a volcanic outbreak, I pour my fluids of life into you, oh … my beloved" Leo.

Ingredients needed for a better understanding for the Couple

Any attempt to enjoy sexuality with your partner to the fullest will not likely work, if the affective and emotional aspects are not satisfactory.

Two people can have sex without having any personal, emotional, or affective ties. This is not what we refer to "making love."

This book, which is titled "Making love with love", seeks to be an instrument that can help couples to develop a tighter bond to each other, it also aims to help develop skills, like improving communication, for the betterment of their relationship.

However, there is no doubt that this will not happen, if there are unresolved conflicts that are affecting the basic fundamentals of mutual understanding.

The necessary ingredients for a better understanding in the couple are: Love, trust, respect, communication, patience, tolerance, time, loyalty, responsibility, compatibility, capacity for forgiveness.

▶ **LOVE:** Love is an intense, deep affection for another person. How do you know if love is present in the relationship with your partner? Could it be just a need to fill the emptiness that you feel? Is it possible that what holds you in the relationship is nothing more than the fear of being alone, or just due to financial needs?

If you have you noticed that when you give a hug to your partner, when you look at her/him, or when you kiss, or hold his/her hand, you feel this "indescribable intense and very special warm feeling inside" that hints to you that, you feel love.

Romantic Love is that wonderful force that makes us feel above our surroundings. It is that supreme feeling that makes your whole being tremble internally. This forceful and pleasant deep satisfaction and yet desire for more of your beloved. Love is an indispensable ingredient for the happiness of the couple. "In the name of love" you can do even what seems to be impossible.

▶ **TRUST:** It is the firm belief in the reliability, truth, ability, and strength of someone. Trust is another indispensable ingredient in the relationship of the couple. Both, in the relationship, must try to give to their partner the reassurance that "one can count on the other", that each one seeks the good for both. Apply in your lives the saying: "I have your back". When a relationship has no trust, the possibility of living in harmony and happiness together is almost nil.

▶ **<u>RESPECT:</u>** A feeling of deep admiration for someone elicited by their abilities, qualities, or achievements. Regard for the feelings, wishes, rights, or traditions of others.

Do you see in your partner a person worthy of your consideration, admiration, and respect?

Think of someone who you know that you undoubtedly respect; now ask yourself if you have been treating your partner with that consideration that it carries respect. If the answer is no, look for the causes and try to correct them.

Mutual respect is too important not to be present in a relationship with love.

▶**<u>COMMUNICATION:</u>** This is also an indispensable ingredient. It is to be expected that in all human relationships, even more so in that of a couple, to have disagreements, bad moments, diversity of opinions, etc. are potential problems. Each one of these can create conflict. Not being able to resolve these conflicts through positive and productive communication will, undoubtedly, cause disturbance to the wellbeing of the couple.

You can refer to the chapter "Essential components for a good communication" (Chapter X)

▶ **<u>PATIENCE:</u>** The capacity to accept or "put up with" delay, trouble, or suffering without getting angry or upset. Any interpersonal relationship requires a good dose of patience, this is true especially for married life.

▶ **<u>TOLERANCE:</u>** Tolerance is the allowing or the acceptance of an action, idea, or person which one dislikes or disagrees with. In the relationship, you both can agree to disagree. Not everyone thinks alike and there should be some room for acceptance and tolerance.

To err is human, we all can make a mistake and, this may require our tolerance to being able to accept what happened, forgive, and move on.

▶ **<u>TIME:</u>** Time is the existence and events that occur in an apparently irreversible succession from the past, through the present, into the future.

It is necessary to give each other time to share and grow together. If it gets busy, "make the time". Though it seems obvious, this is also an important and necessary part of a successful relationship. Put the time to keep the fire of love alive. Both of you should continue to cultivate the land where you planted the seeds of love, and where the roots of your love are still ready to keep growing.

▶**LOYALTY:** Is the faithfulness owed by duty, by a pledge, by promise, or by choice. Our society has promoted a monogamous relationship. Most married couples and committed relationships expect exclusivity in their sexual intimacy. Loyalty in the relationship is faithfulness in keeping your promises. The feeling that you can rely on each other. Some may both agree to an open relationship.

▶ **RESPONSIBILITY:** It is something you are required to do as an upstanding member of a community, it implies good judgment and the ability to act correctly and make decisions on your own. One, or both of you, will need to be the providers. At least one of you would have to work for an income to pay the expenses involved in living independently. Either or both should see that the house chores, the welfare of children, the daily schedule, and the maintenance of certain house rules get done. It all tends to work better when both, in the couple, know what their responsibilities are.

▶ **COMPATIBILITY:** Described as the state in which two entities can exist or occur together without problems or conflict; a feeling of sympathy, friendship, like-mindedness that bond the two of them. Another point that seems obvious, but sometimes can be overlooked.

- How well do you know your partner and, how at ease do you feel sharing activities together?
- Do you share similar likings?
- Do you enjoy fun activities together?
- Do you have similar goals in life?
- Do you have a similar scale of values?
- What is good for one, is it good or bad for the other?
- Do you both believe in the same God and live your religion in the same way?
- Do you both have a similar philosophy of life?

If you realize you are both mostly compatible, great. If in many aspects you are not compatible, how important are those? With love, understanding and compromise the lack of compatibility in many aspects can be overcome if there is a mutual desire to help each other and complement each other.

▶ **<u>CAPACITY OF FORGIVENESS:</u>** Forgiveness is the intentional and voluntary process by which one who may initially feel victimized, undergoes a change in feelings and attitude regarding a given offense, and overcomes negative emotions such as resentment and vengeance. Whether the given offense was real or imaginary, when a person does not have the ability for forgiveness, he or she may have much difficulty maintaining a satisfactory relationship. Sometimes it may be necessary to forgive yourself, and other times to forgive your partner. Putting into practice forgiveness is the only way to heal an emotional scar.

Make an analysis of everything mentioned above. If you identify that one or more of these important points are missing in your relationship, you and your partner should take the decision to overcome those problems right now.

Developing good communication skills will likely lead to a better understanding and improve your relationship. Including the necessary ingredients for a good relationship in your life can increase the chance to live together in harmony and happiness.

XIII

Suggestions and Comments

Let us open the doors, so that together, as a couple, you both embark on the journey to discover greater fulfillment in your sexuality.

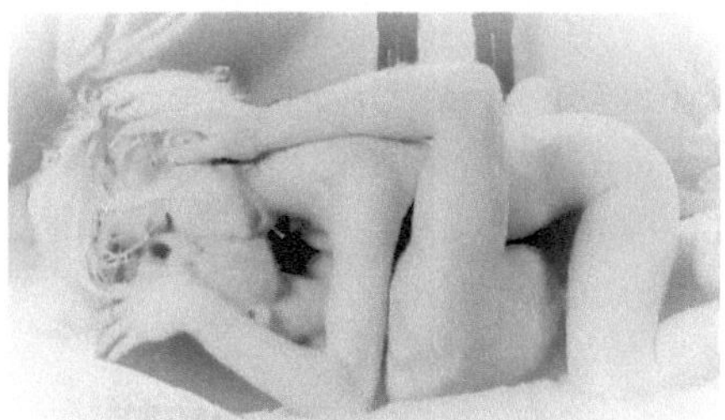

By "making love with love", what we seek is: *"To Honor each other and build a bridge between our bodies, our HEARTS and our spirits"*. We seek to promote a harmonious flow of positive emotions…

By "making love with love," one should understand that, when it comes to sexual intimacy, the mutual surrender and giving is complete.

Break free from prejudices, censures, and fears. All forms of caressing are allowed and are manifestations of your love. In a trusting manner, both of you, exercising your full freedom, can give yourself to the being you love…

The more open and vulnerable you place yourself in front of your partner, the greater will be the growth of the trust between the two.

To walk towards "giving each other completely", towards a full surrender, by making love with love, trust in your partner should be deposited, and you could give yourself permission to manifest your love without inhibitions, and freely.

In love "anything goes", as long as, there is an
atmosphere of consideration, respect, and desire to
mutually accommodate to the needs of your partner.

The most important organ, in the mission of making love, is the brain. The emotional aspect takes more than half the success of satisfaction.

For the <u>man</u>, it is especially important that his partner shows him <u>respect, appreciation, and passion.</u>

On the other hand, for the <u>woman</u> it is especially important that her partner shows that he <u>loves</u> her, he is there to <u>protect</u> her, and that he <u>admires</u> her beauty.

"Making love" starts long before they are physically together. They both miss each other, they reminisce about the moments of complete surrender they shared, and imagine what they will do when they get together again.

They treat each other with affection, sweetness, and consideration. They flirt and are playful, they share loving words and loving gestures.

Finally, in the privacy, where they feel comfortable, they will start with lusty looks, caresses, kisses, and complete surrender, while feeling a growing passion that invades them.

Having a good predisposition and open mind to learn new techniques of how to please your partner can come in handy.

Try not close the door of discovery and, within an environment of trust-and-love, explore different and multiple ways to indulge each other.

Having a good sense of humor can be most helpful for the couple, having the confidence to laugh at each other without taking offense, having the ability not to take everything seriously, being able to feel relaxed and comfortable sharing a good laugh can be a "boost" for love.

- ♥ You should look for a complete ABANDONMENT of one towards the other.
- ♥ Total surrender WITHOUT PREJUDICES, nor conditions.
- ♥ Get to the point of feeling COMFORTABLE to be able to suggest innovations.
- ♥ Free yourself from fears that can slow your initiative down.
- ♥ Free yourself from the anxiety of feeling rejected.
- ♥ Free yourself from the fear of not being able to satisfy your mate.

♥ Come to feel that EVERYTHING YOU GIVE AND RECEIVE IS A PRODUCT OF THE EXPRESSION OF THIS IMMENSE LOVE YOU HAVE FOR EACH OTHER.

♥ Don't feel ashamed.

♥ Venture out to try new things.

♥ Be creative, and both of you do your part to participate willingly.

♥ DO NOT STAY IN A RECEPTIVE MODE ONLY and take the active role.

♥ Take the initiative to express your love with passion and fire.

♥ Try to feel like you both are totally delivering to each other your bodies, emotions, and thoughts.

When you are making love with love you are giving each other the following message:

"It is so grand the love that I have for you, that
the passion with force floods my senses, provoking
an overflow of positive emotions leading to a total
surrender of my being... "Love of my life"...
sharing with you is a bit of heaven on earth".

Helpful Comments about Human Behavior:

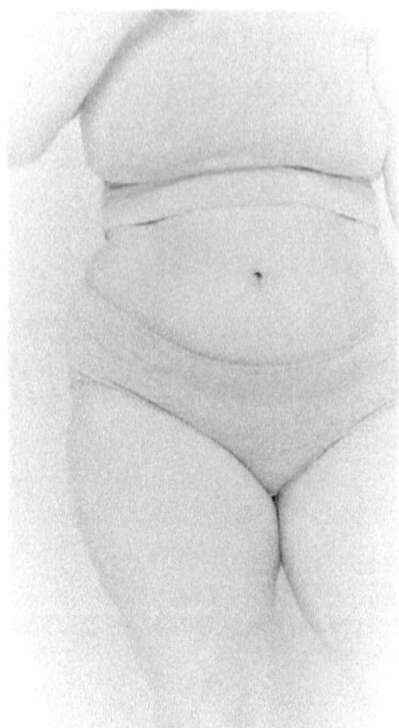

▶ "Your body is perfect, just like it is". To have a positive self-image will allow you to take better care of yourself and others. **To better yourself is a good thing** but do not let this damage your self-esteem. If someone does not like you or accept you the way you are, you might be with the wrong person. Or vice versa.

"Love and accept yourself as you are, this is the
first step towards a happy relationship".

▶ You are who you think you are, the image that you have of yourself is the image that you project to others.

▶ In our mind, and without realizing it, we have that part of us that is constantly judging us, likewise, this part is constantly judging everyone else. When we find ourselves at fault, which we frequently do, we punish ourselves, and become the main obstacle to reaching our own peace and happiness.

▶ We often have emotional wounds that, we carry all the way from childhood, and an important way to heal them is through forgiveness, towards ourselves and towards those who, in our perception, were the ones that hurt us in some way.

We may believe that we cannot forgive, it may be because of pride that gets in the way. We were born with the ability to forgive, we just must start practicing it and, with time, it will become something natural and automatic.

The main beneficiary of the act of forgiveness is the one who forgives, as it will free that person of the negative charge that him or her has been carrying for years.

▶ **In all relationship there are two halves, you are only responsible for your half.**

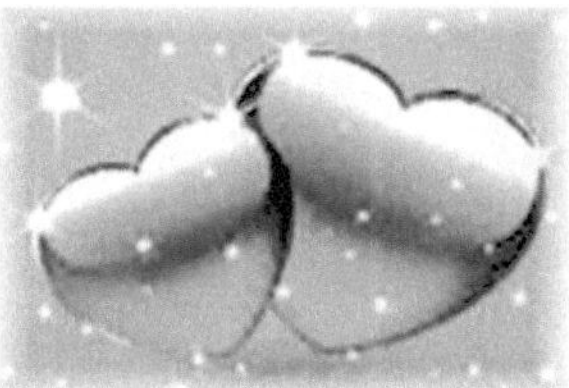

▶ If you think that you will find your happiness in another person, if you think that your happiness depends on your mate, you are mistaken.

Nobody can "make you happy", your happiness is the result of the love that comes out of yourself.

▶ Communication based on respect and love is the key to keep love alive.

▶ If you treat your partner with respect and love, who benefits? Yourself. You take care of sanitizing and improving your half of the relationship and your chances of a happy relationship will be much greater.

▶ Fool is the one that expects a different result every time, but keeps doing the same, over, and over again. Without realizing many have done this. If you expect a different result, be sure to do things differently.

▶ If you are the type of person who believes that you are always right, besides the fact that nobody is always correct (to err is human), this conduct may negatively affect your relationship. Only when a person recognizes that he/she is wrong, then the option of changing is possible. By correcting a mistake, we have the option to learn and to grow.

▶ Love has no obligations, it has no expectations, it is based on respect, compassion, responsibility, kindness, and unconditional giving. But it does not mean that you let the other one walk all over you and do nothing about it. Because you also love yourself you should not allow others to mistreat you either. Love is not about abstract definitions… it is about action. The only way to grow in love is by taking the action to give and receive.

▶ In the couple relationship, we have the option of creating conflict and making of the relationship a battlefield or not. Trying to control or manipulate the other may be erroneously our focus of attention.

On the other hand, we also have the option of making our partner our "playmate" with whom we play together, not against each other. It is not about winning or losing, it is all about having a good time, so we both win.

▶ If we think we are looking for love, but what we are looking for someone who needs us, someone to control and manipulate, then we are not looking for love. It is better to be with someone who wants to be with you and not someone who needs to be with you.

▶ Attitudes of jealousy, possessiveness and selfishness will only distant your partner. Trying to control or manipulate your partner will create a defensive attitude in your partner. If there is no harmony in your relationship think of the possibility that you may be the one at fault.

▶ Having a generous attitude with love towards your partner will likely be an unspoken invitation for the other to do the same.

▶ You may not have control of what happens around you or what happens to you, but you can control your own thoughts and actions. One of the keys to having a wonderful life is to learn to control your own reactions and, remember that you are responsible for what you think, do, and speak.

▶ When it comes to "Making love": give yourself to each other completely, play together with interest and enthusiasm. Make your love affair an adventure of pleasure, love, and surrender. Both of you will remain, not only satisfied, but more united.

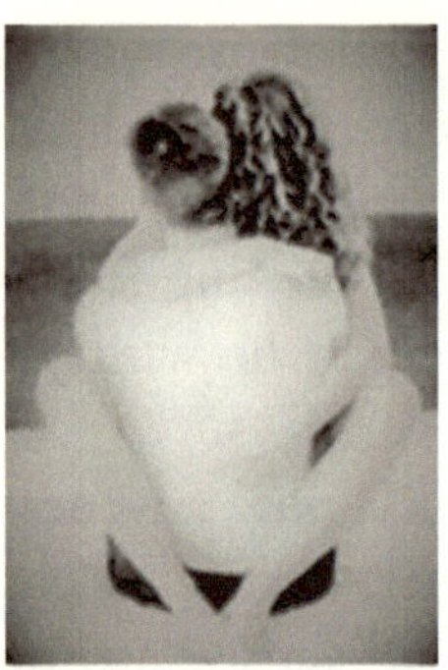

▶ Tomorrow when you wake up, and equally all days to come from here on, tell yourself: Today, like all the other days, I will do something nice for my partner to place a sweet smile on his/her face.

Now, when BOTH in the relationship do the same… ♥♥♥♥♥ Both will be smiling.

XIV

Sexual Anatomy and Physiology

Only basic and easy to understand descriptions will be provided for the purpose of this presentation.

<u>The sexual anatomy of the male:</u> The copulatory and reproductive organ of the man has, the visible part that is, the penis and the scrotal bags, where the testicles are located. Internally there are the canaliculi that communicate the testicles with the penis and to the exterior.

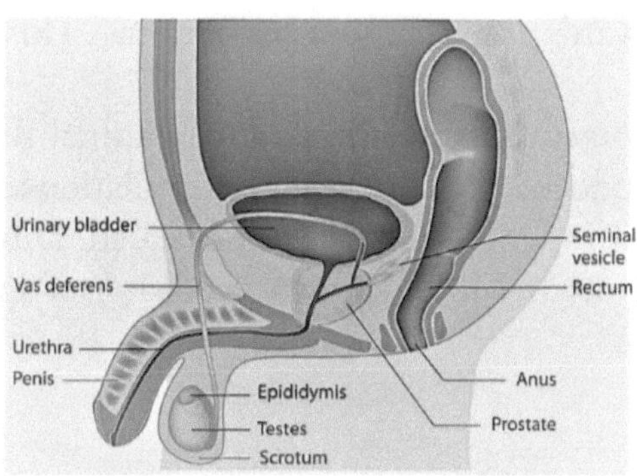

We also find the prostate at the base of the bladder which also has important sexual functions.

The testicles are responsible for producing the male hormone called Testosterone, in addition to forming sperm to be expelled during ejaculation.

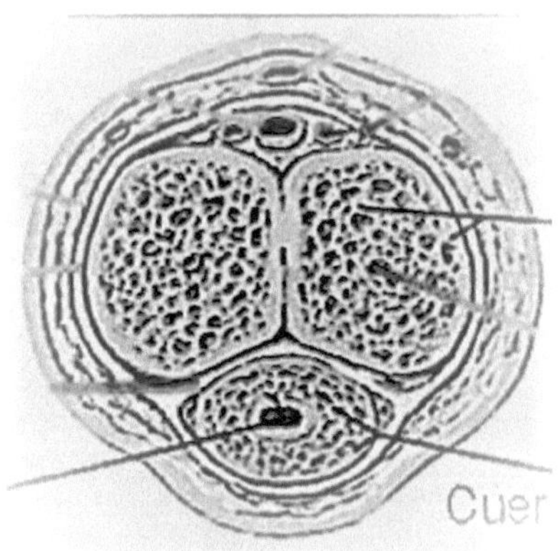

A tangential section of the penis shows the cavernous and spongy bodies that, when they get filled with blood, an erection occurs. In the midline we find the urethra, tube through which urine is eliminated and, also sperm during ejaculation.

During sexual stimulation, (visual, auditory, tactile, gustatory, olfactory, or just some erotic thought), there will be an increased blood flow to the

penis, towards the corpora cavernosa. This will produce the erection.

Simultaneously, during stimulation, seminal fluid, and sperm starts being produced. As the sexual stimulation continues some seminal fluid with sperm can start to be released. During the climax, ejaculation will occur with a sudden expulsion of sperm and semi-nal fluid.

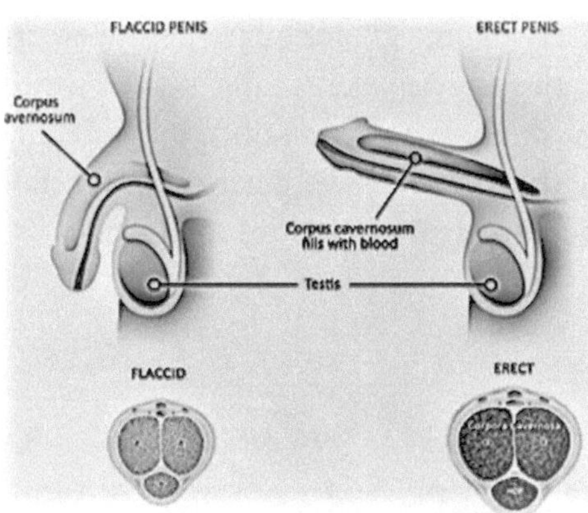

In general, a man gets sexually aroused more easily and faster than a woman.

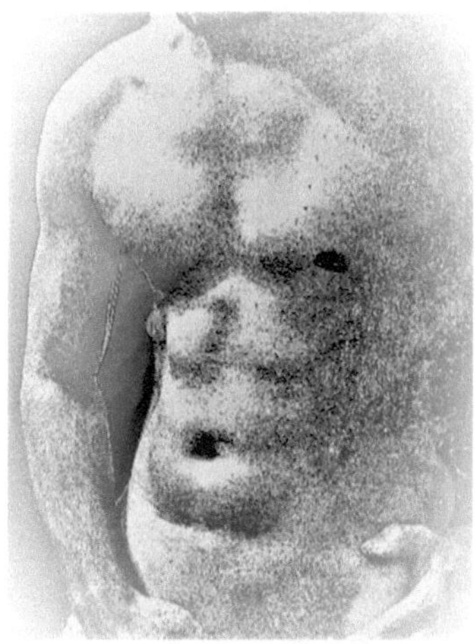

The physical and instinctive nature can frequently prevail over the rational or emotional aspects. Several are the reasons including: the high level of testosterone, the procreation instinct for the preservation of the species, in addition to the cultural conditioning.

Several factors intervene for an adequate penile erection.
- Anatomic: the arteries, veins, and nerve stimulation,
- Psychological: anxiety, depression, self-esteem,
- Situational: partner-related, performance related,
- Functional: endocrine (testosterone level).

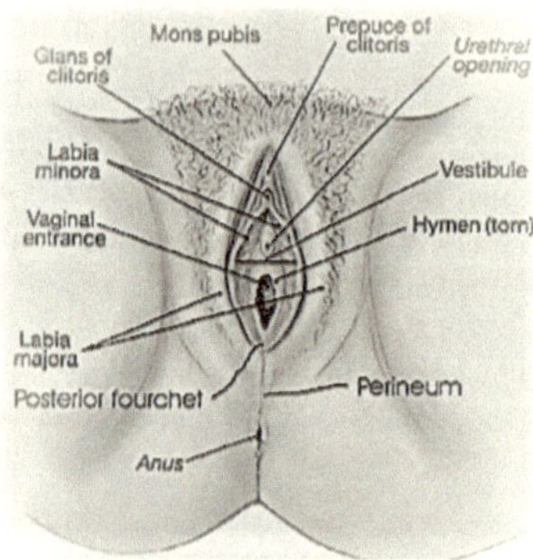

<u>Sexual anatomy of women:</u> The vulva is the global term that describes all the structures that make the **female** external **genitalia**.

The components of the **vulva** are the mons pubis, labia majora, labia minora, clitoris, vestibular bulbs, vulva vestibule, Bartholin›s glands, Skene›s glands, urethra, and **vaginal** opening.

At the end of the vaginal canal the cervix (The lower, narrow end of the uterus that forms a canal between the uterus and vagina) is found.

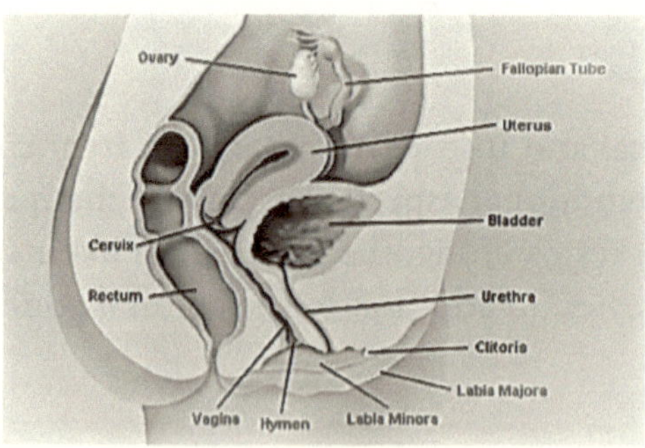

Sexual arousal and stimulation, in women, leads to the increment of secretion of lubricating vaginal fluid and, the pelvic muscles relax, facilitating the penetration. The clitoris fills up of blood, in addition to an increment of blood flow to the entire pelvis. The clitoris can get engorged and become more sensitive.

The rise in the level of sexual arousal tends to be slower for women than for men, but it can stay, at a high arousal level, by considerably longer periods of time, allowing the possibility of multiple orgasms.

In general, the emotional component of the sexual desire tends to be much greater in women than in men.

As sexual arousal and stimulation continues an orgasm can occur.

An orgasm is the series of muscle contractions in the genital region that is accompanied by sudden release of endorphins. An orgasm is the physical and emotional sensation usually experienced at the peak of sexual excitation.

This wonderful experience is described in multiple ways including: "an uninhibited release of control and self-consciousness", "It's a buildup of tension that arches your back and curls your toes, almost like a clenching feeling, and just when you think you cannot take it anymore, suddenly all that tension is released and pulses throughout your body. It's the best relief.", etc., etc.

SEXUAL RELATIONSHIPS DURING SPECIAL TIMES:

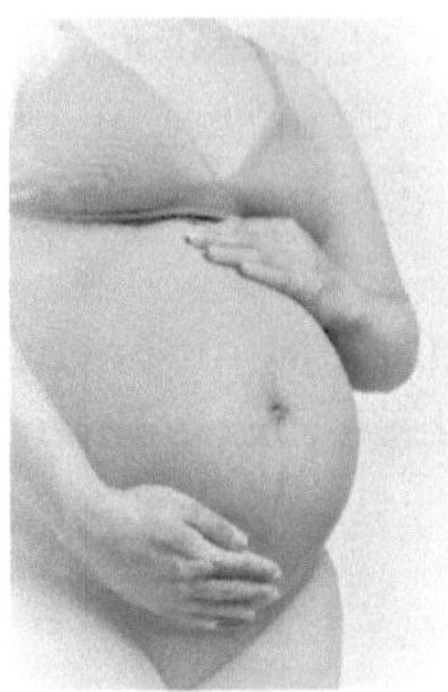

- ▶ **During pregnancy**: In a <u>normal</u> pregnancy you can have sex throughout the pregnancy until just before the day of delivery. There is no particular risk for the baby, during sex, in a normal pregnancy.

  As it can be understood, for logistical reasons, as the pregnancy progresses and the womb grows, the man will no longer be able to lean on his partner, and the option will be to approach from a front position without putting pressure on her belly, from behind or from a side. In any case, it will be advisable to consult with the obstetrician who will determine if the pregnancy is normal, and if there are no risks for each case.

- ▶ **During menstruation**: Except for the possible discomfort for her, especially if her periods come with pain and abdominal bloating; or in the case of disgust by the presence of blood in the vagina that could have the spouse, there is no health contraindication to be able to have intercourse during menstruation. The risk of pregnancy during this time is much lower. To have sexual intercourse at this time will be an option for the couple to decide, but it is considered normal and acceptable by most. If the couple prefer, they could use a condom.

▶ **Sex after menopause**: You can enjoy sexual intercourse practically throughout the adult life, age is not a limitation by itself.

The menopause occurs when women stop producing the female hormone called Estrogen. It can be natural or after a surgery that removes the ovaries. As a result of the lack of female hormones, several changes can occur such as cessation of menstruation, the inability to get pregnant anymore, some emotional changes, hot flashes, decreased vaginal fluid secretion, etc.

The low estrogen levels can be a cause of low sexual desire (libido), as well as vaginal dryness. If this gets in the way of enjoying sex, visit with your doctor about it.

On the other hand, there are women that will increase their sexual desire, level of arousal, and satisfaction when they understand that they are at no risk of getting pregnant, and that they will no longer have any more vaginal bleeding.

Sexual Fantasies

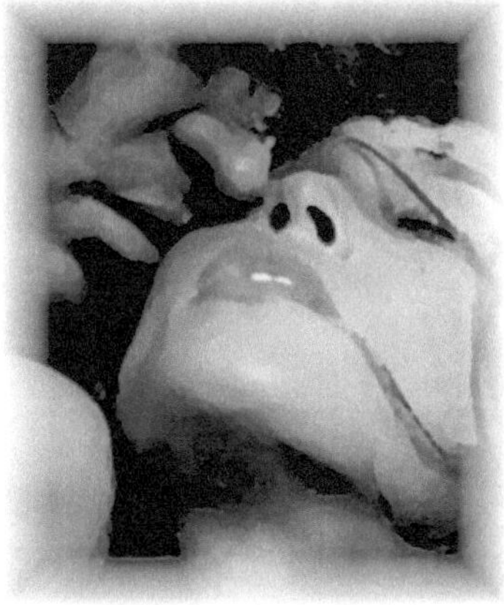

Fantasy is a dream, it is something imaginary, not real. Like dreams, you have no control in them and, you can let your imagination run wild, free without censorship. A sexual fantasy is any mental image, thought, or story that turns you on; erotic daydreaming that provides sexual arousal in the person who imagines it. The great thing about fantasies is that they do not have to mix with your real-life ethics and beliefs.

Most of these fantasies will be about sexual situations or activities that the individual may have never experienced, and that generally has no intention of carrying them out into reality. Although, as long as the fantasy is consensual, freely given, reversible, informed, enthusiastic, and specific, the couple can choose to act it out.

No matter what your dream is in fantasyland, remember that your private thoughts do not define you, and that it is okay to have sexual fantasies that conflict with who you believe yourself to be in real life.

Your fantasy life is your fantasy life, until and unless you choose to make it into more. Whether the situations you picture in your mind are tame or wild, sexual imagination can be a positive contributor of joy and excitement.

To have sexual fantasies can be a positive and harmless activity unless they interfere negatively with the conduct of the person or that this is the only source of sexual stimulation.

Fantasies can be provoked voluntarily in the person's mind, as well as appear involuntarily. Other times, the erotic reverie is based in an experience in the past that the individual wants to recreate in his/her mind.

Examples of sexual fantasies can include:
- Having sex with a stranger,
- Having homosexual activities with other partners,
- Sex in unusual places,

- Sex with multiple partners at the same time,
- Being taken by force,
- Reminiscing of previous sexual contacts,
- Group sex,
- Dominating the sex partner,
- Sex in public or semipublic with the risk of getting caught,
- Blindfolded sex,
- Dressing up costumes for sex,
- Role playing.

Some people worry about the content of their fantasies, they may even feel guilty of imagining certain things. There may be some cultural and moral conflicts about the fantasies. Individuals need to know that, as long as they are imaginary and increase their sexual pleasure, they can feel free to enjoy them.

Whether to share your fantasy or not is a personal decision but, be aware that the partner may not understand nor appreciate the content of it. On the other hand, if there was a "Fantasy" that both, in the couple, want to make it into reality, while no harm to self or third parties can occur, then enjoy them.

Sexual fantasies are very personal, only the individual who is having the fantasy knows of its existence, in general and, in the vast majority of cases, they may better remain very intimate and private.

Openly sharing sexual fantasies could cause unnecessary misunderstandings, jealousy, or grudges with your partner.

However, on some occasions, sharing sexual fantasies with your partner can be positive and increase the sexual desire of both, it remains to use the good judgment to know when and what fantasies to share.

Discovering your Body

Many women have been through many events, including giving birth to children without knowing "how it looks down there".

Why is it important to know your own body and how it feels touching certain parts? It is a good idea to discover, if you already do not know, how it feels to touch certain parts of your body and with different types of stimuli.

Marcela (imaginary name) tells us something about her self-discovery experience:

"One fine day I decided, in the privacy of my own bedroom, to observe my most intimate parts. The room temperature was pleasant, I decided to undress completely, I found a small mirror and proceeded to sit on the bed with my legs spread and the mirror reflecting my private areas. It was quite a nice experience and I was able to identify all the different parts, the clitoris, the labia and, the vaginal canal. With my lubricated finger, I touched each one of these parts. I noticed a pleasant sensation when I gently slid my fingers by my vaginal lips. I particularly liked it when, firmly, I pressed on the clitoris. I tried all that came to my imagination. I even introduced, first one, and then several fingers in my vagina, I even tried one finger in the back door. Although I was alone, I giggled and had so much fun. With the insatiable curiosity that it got in me, I continued my exploration. I took longer time in some areas because it felt delicious. I noticed something interesting when I put two fingers inside my vagina, and I squeezed them. I felt the strength of these muscles on the sides of the fingers, and likewise it felt nice in my vagina. Later I learned that strengthening these muscles can increase my pleasure and my partners… I proposed to exercise regularly… LOL. By the time I realized, two hours had passed."

You could explore yourself, as Marcela did, and he could also explore other areas of his body. One of the largest organs in the body is the skin. Touch and caress all the parts that are to your reach and your imagination allows, then see which are the most sensitive areas, you can get back to them or tell your partner to do it for you.

XVII

Masturbation

The erotic stimulation of one's own genital organs that commonly results in an **orgasm**. It usually can be achieved by manual or by instrumental manipulation of the genitalia or other body parts.

Most of the time accompanied by sexual fantasies and has the purpose of self-sexual gratification.

Talking about this topic can sometimes be quite difficult, some people may even consider masturbation as something "forbidden, bad, or dirty". Well, if you have reached this part of the book, likely it is because you have the desire to learn more, and to open the doors to knowledge about healthy sexuality.

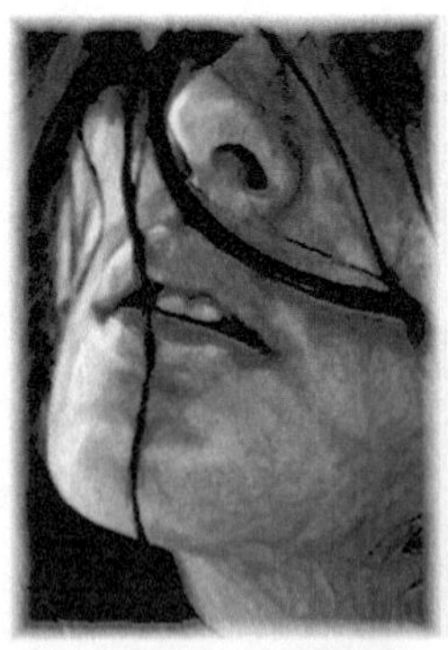

Most men and women have, at one point or another, practiced masturbation. Masturbation is considered a normal activity in the development of human sexuality. Studies have shown that around 90% of men and 63% of women have masturbated regularly or at some stage of their lifetime.

Features are not limited to stress relief in the absence of a partner, but also, people get to know their preferences better. They can develop more pleasant techniques through personal experimentation.

There are many myths and misinformation about masturbation, like young boys were told it can cause blindness, or others have said it can cause insanity, it weakens the person, will not let a person concentrate, will give you a headache etc., etc. Of course, all these are false.

It is important to understand that masturbation does not cause any problems unless it goes against the individual's own morals and affects them negatively.

Masturbation can be contemplated as an excellent opportunity for self-education.

The attitude towards masturbation should be open and calm, discarding feelings of anxiety, and guilt.

Self-eroticism is not limited to self-stimulation of your genitals. There are many other forms of self-erotic experiences such as: taking a prolonged bath with aromatic substances, feel the gentle breeze on sun-kissed skin lying by the ocean, feel the raindrops on your face in a summer hot day, etc.

Those who accept masturbation as a natural act will be able to feel reassured and practice it individually or in a shared way with their partner.

Mutually masturbating can be something exciting and enjoyable as well as educational, it can be one more way to increase sexual enjoyment with your partner.

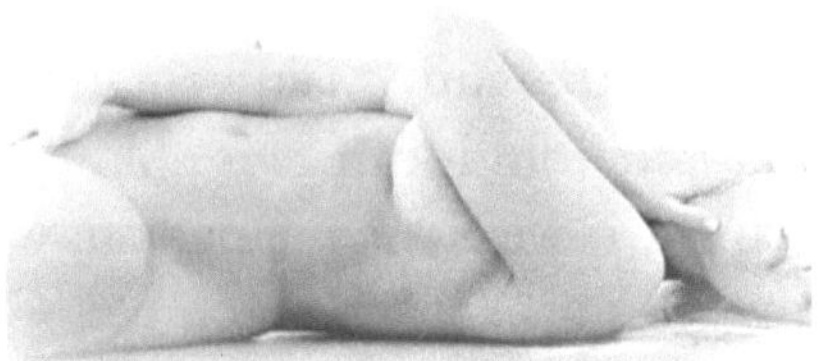

Masturbating, without guilt feelings, can help people feel liberated to express their sexuality.

Furthermore, masturbation can be an alternative to intercourse for the couple, in special situations such as: in the last stage of pregnancy, postpartum, if one is convalescing for health reasons, or even in case of excessive physical exhaustion.

Masturbation can be a positive experience for the person, but it is not considered indispensable in the development of sexuality for the individual or the couple, it is simply optional.

Right to Sexual Satisfaction:

The ability to achieve pleasure depends mainly on the attitude and mental predisposition of the person, him, or herself. The person hopefully should feel that it is his/her right to experience sexual pleasure.

The human being must realize that enjoying sexuality and achieving pleasure is beneficial, not only physically, but also mentally, and emotionally.

You can make use of erotic fantasies, free yourself to think of anything that sexually arouses you. Remember that this is your moment of pleasure.

Just touching or rubbing the genital area may not bring sexual stimulation, it will require the combination of locating the erogenous zones, daydreaming in sexual fantasy, and having the delivered intent to provoke yourself the sexual pleasure desired. It is like working with a concrete goal in mind.

XVIII

Oral Sex

The sexual activity in which the genitals of one partner are stimulated by the mouth of the other; it is called fellatio when performed to a man, and cunnilingus when performed to a woman.

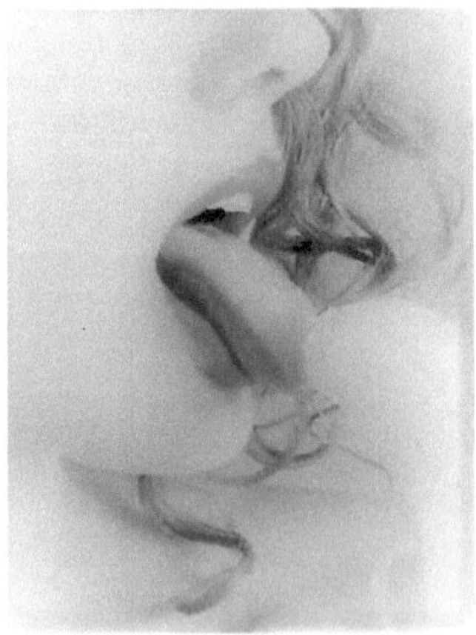

When a couple loves each other, both seek to make each other happy, whereby giving pleasure to the partner will give a lot of satisfaction to the one who gives as well as the one who receives.

Most people seem to accept and enjoy oral sex, yet there is still those few who, due to false fears and misinformation, see it as something "bad" (which is not), and that on the contrary, it helps the bonding and complementation of the couple.

However, it is worth mentioning that oral sex, like other forms of sexual manifestation, are optional for each couple and for each individual.

There is no "recipe" that works for all, since each person is different, but being gentle and slow, approaching the areas of less sensitivity to the most erogenous areas can help.

While communication is the basis of a positive experience in intimacy, sometimes trying to "explain" at the very moment of performing the action can backfire. It may affect the flow and cause distraction, having to be giving instructions in the moment of intimacy, and there may be those who may feel offended.

Positive reinforcement when something you feel is pleasurable, non-verbal communication in those moments of pleasure should be more like gestures or brief comments. Another alternative is to share likes and dislikes at a different time. Oral sex can increase sexual pleasure largely, and most couples enjoy giving and receiving it.

*"My adorable lady, your sensuality intoxicates
me and, your scent makes me pleasantly crazy.
When I place my head in between your naked
and well contoured legs, when my lips touch your
tender labia, when my frenzy tongue explores your
interior and savors your sweets fluids, when I
listen you moaning and, I feel you trembling full
of pleasure… not only do I feel immensely aroused,
but it also makes me so happy to know and deeply
sense that you are mine… sweet beloved "*

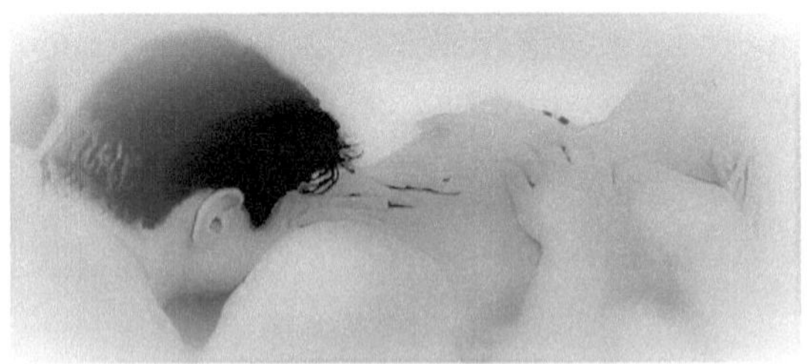

Oral sex in the couple, not only helps them to enjoy more sexual pleasure, but it can also increment the bonding by sharing something so intimate.

Useful suggestions for giving him oral sex:

◊ Oral sex goes beyond just concentrating on the penis.

◊ Apart from using the mouth, lips, and tongue, you can use hands to simultaneously stimulate other parts of the genital region or the body.

◊ The psychological and emotional aspect is quite important. Getting oral sex, for him, can denote acceptance, passion, love, surrender, desire, manifestation of wanting to satisfy him, well… it is very positive.

◊ The most sensitive erogenous zones can include the head of the penis, the frenulum, found immediately below the head of the penis, and the middle raphe that, runs along the lower part of the penis and continues along the midline to the region of the anus. The perineum, which is the part that is between the anus and the base of the penis, is also quite sensitive.

◊ The stimulation of all these erogenous zones will bring more pleasure to your partner, you can kiss, lick, gently suck, gently slide your tongue and lips, rubbing, even soft biting, etc. Good lubrication can increase the pleasant sensation. The penis can take quite a bit of local pressure, rubbing, even gentle "slapping", but the testicles are more delicate to local trauma and need more gentle handling. The penis is particularly pleasantly sensitive to squeezing.

◊ You can initially kiss and caress the entire genital area to finally end on the penis. Think of the penis as your favorite "Lollipop", and delight yourself by savoring it, licking it, kissing it, and sucking it gently.

◊ Finally, when you proceed to put the penis in the mouth, avoid scratching with the teeth, this is achieved by inverting the lips a little inwards and opening the mouth wide enough to avoid contact of the teeth against the penis.

◊ With good lubrication and a constant suction slide in and out.

◊ Simultaneously, with your tongue, you can caress the lower part of the penis producing a very pleasant stimulation for your partner.

◊ While doing as suggested the above, you can with your hands caress the buttocks of your partner, caress the testicles delicately, exerting gentle pressure.

◊ You can also use your hand on the base of the penis gently trapping around it, forming a kind of "tunnel". The walls of this "tunnel" will then include internal part of the cheeks, her lips closing in a ring around the penis and the hand. With good lubrication can slide in and out, making a longer "tunnel" in this way. This variant It also has the advantage that allows women to exercise better control in the depth of the penetration of the penis in the mouth.

◊ When you feel more audacious, and want to give your male partner a surprise, you can massage his prostate. To achieve this, lubricate a finger well and slowly insert it in his anus; the prostate is about 5 cm. (2") inside towards the anterior wall. You can apply pressure directly and rub in small circles.

◊ A few words about semen. It is the viscous whitish fluid of the male reproductive tract consisting of spermatozoa suspended in secretions of the accessory glands (as of the prostate and Cowper's glands). It is optional, whether the lady wants to swallow it or not. Many couples enjoy doing it this way because they feel that the degree of intimacy increases, but other couples prefer not to.

◊ Regarding the position, any position you choose will work, if both of you are comfortable.

◊ About the penetration depth of the penis in mouth, the man must be careful not to penetrate more than what the partner can tolerate, and best would be if the woman who has control in this matter. She can decide, according to her comfort, and to how sensitive her gaging reflex is, how deep to put it in. Women can learn to control the gaging reflex, and it is important to know that the satisfaction of oral sex is not limited to depth of the penetration rather than to everything else above mentioned.

◊ Oral sex is a manifestation of love and lust, ideally both will enjoy it, giving as well as receiving.

◊ Among other benefits of oral sex include Helping to achieve a better erection of the penis, and to achieve an orgasm without penetration. When He feels exhausted from work, oral sex, in conjunction with manual stimulation, can be a very good way to give sexual pleasure to your loved one.

Useful information for giving her Oral Sex:

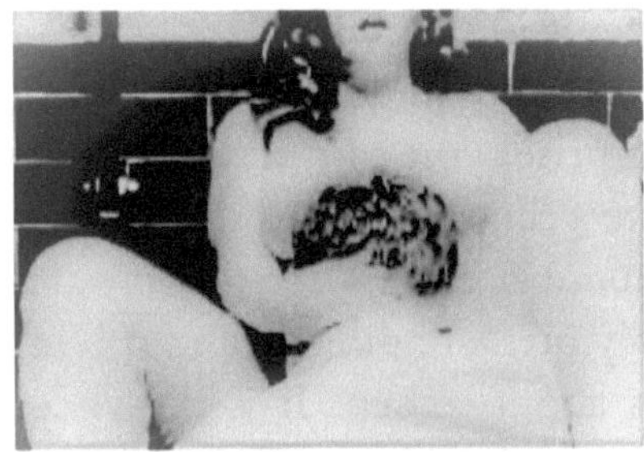

♥ Giving your wife oral sex is one of the most wonderful things you can do for her. It makes her feel loved, admired, sexy, and of course can help her reach an orgasm.

♥ Some women say that it is exciting for them to know that their partner finds it "delicious".

♥ Most women are shy when it comes to their own body, it will be good that she can feel trusting enough to relax and enjoy, in addition to allowing her partner to place comfortably his head between her legs.

As obvious as it may be, men may need to shave and clip nails before going down there.

♥ Most women appreciate sweet words and affection during intimacy, others prefer more roughness, but generally women are more receptive to "verbal love" than men.

♥ The Clitoris is usually the most sensitive part for most women. That little fleshy bump above the opening of the vagina is full of nerve endings that make it overly sensitive to touch.

♥ An essential requirement is delicacy, specially at the beginning; the stimulus can slowly increase in intensity and progressively advance. The sequence of starting first with affection, move on to caresses and kisses, only then approach the genital area to finally reach the clitoris will usually be welcome. Lubrication can help to increase her pleasure.

♥ Some women agree that "almost everything he does feels great" if the attention starts with initial delicacy, then, progressively, and slowly, raises up in intensity. It will likely feel very pleasant when he licks, kisses, and sucks on the labia, the entrance to the vagina, the clitoris, and the anal area.

♥ Whichever position that is comfortable for both of you will be appropriate. As a suggestion: She can lay on the edge of the bed, transverse, facing up, and with the knees bent and separated, he positions himself at the edge of the bed and has direct access to the entire area, He also has his hands free to caress her.

♥ Position "69" (one's head between the legs of the other simultaneously) will allow both to give each other oral sex. When she is on top, she can control the depth and force of the penetration of the penis in her mouth. Him on top can also be very pleasant for both. Lying sideways in position "69" is a more rested position for both. In short, the position will depend on the creativity of both, and remember "everything goes".

♥ Some suggestions for the use the tongue on his beloved include, with the tongue relaxed, slide it from bottom to top licking the labia up to the clitoris, then parting the vaginal lips with the fingers, now he can lick all the exposed area from top to bottom and vice versa. By stiffening his tongue, he will be able to insert it into the vagina, then when she is already more excited lick the clitoris and combine with suctions from all parts.

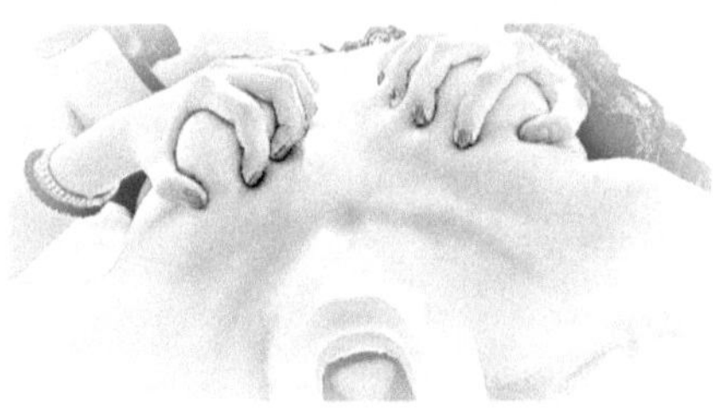

♥ A pleasant stimulus can consist of combining clitoral suction, and simultaneously with the tongue in a circular motion press against the clitoris.

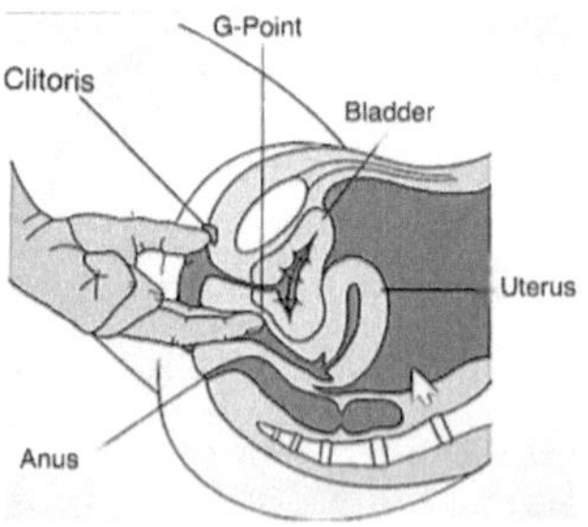

♥ Using the fingers (be sure to be with nails clipped or use latex gloves) he can increase the level of excitation, he will proceed to introduce them (one, two or more as the vagina and her liking allows) in the lubricated vagina then, palm up, do a rhythmic movement of forward bending the finger to stimulate the G-spot (on the anterior wall of the vagina, about 4 cm. vaginal opening). This rugged area is rich in nerve endings.

♥ As an additive, stimulating and caressing the anus can increase the level of stimulation and pleasure for some people. Initially delicately circularly at the entrance, then, and with good lubrication, insert a finger. At first without moving, it and then delicately moving it in circular motion, plus slide in and out.

♥ How long should I do oral sex? Until she tells you to interrupt.

♥ Some will prefer to have deem light, others indicate they want enough light to see the body of their beloved.

♥ For more enjoyment He could pay attention to her messages, either verbally, or by her moans, or the depth of her breathing, or her movements, to perceive her acceptance. When she appears to show acceptance, verbalizing it or actions like lifting your hips towards the focus of stimuli, or pressing her genitalia against him, the partner can try to continue the same stimulus to raise her level of enjoyment even more.

Oral sex can be one of the most exciting experiences for the couple. Focus on your partner's pleasure and make it a memorable experience. Practice often, be receptive to the feedback signs, and especially enjoy it.

XIX

Sexual Positions

It is of utmost importance, for the benefit of the relationship, to maintain a high level of interest in intimacy, and to preserve alive the fire of passion. Many factors that help in this task including:
- Spontaneity,
- Variability,
- Creativity, and especially
- the feeling of Freedom to be able to suggest and proceed with innovations in "the bedroom games" of your own privacy.

In the "Kama Sutra", an ancient Indian Sanskrit text on sexuality, eroticism, and emotional fulfillment in life, it is claimed that there are more than 500 possible positions to make love. According to this source, the only limitation is in the imagination of the couple, and the physical condition thereof.

Curiosity, creativity, willingness to try new things, spontaneity, trust, sense of adventure, personal preferences, vivid imagination can all contribute to trying and enjoy different positions.

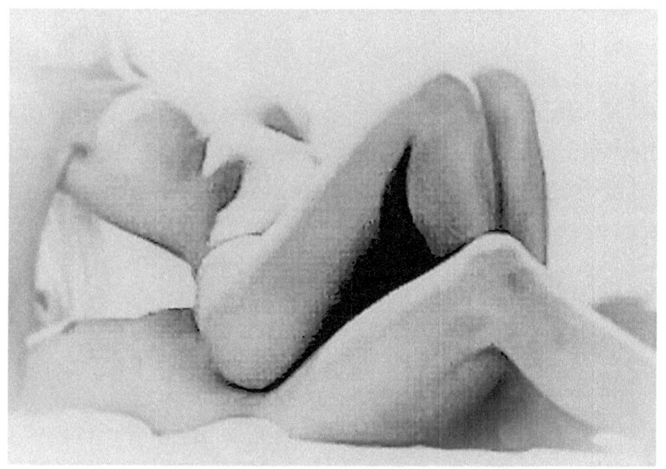

Making *Love* with *Love*

Sex Toys

It may be possible that by using sex toys, expanding the boundaries of sexuality, you could stimulate the senses, excite desires, fulfill fantasies, and spend hours of pleasure in a new world that you and your partner can create.

A better sex life depends on having "in the bedroom" creativity, trust, open communication, and variety. Expanding the boundaries of intimacy, for the couple, it can be a fun trip, and add pleasure for both.

Often there is a resistance of the idea of incorporating "Sex toys" in the relationship. Among some false myths we have:
- "I can get addicted to sex toys."
- "I will no longer be able to have an orgasm without the use of toys."
- "It's only for lonely women."
- "I will no longer be able to enjoy sexual intercourse without toys."
- "It can replace the need for a partner."

Sex therapists claim that, in so many years of practice, they have not seen problems like these.

One of the most fascinating things about Human Sexuality is the ability to have creativity and variety. A healthy curiosity it is part of the human being.

"Sex toys" can be a positive addition in the art of love making for the couple. They can open the door to use them to increase variety, mischief and so on to break the monotony that frequently occur in many couples.

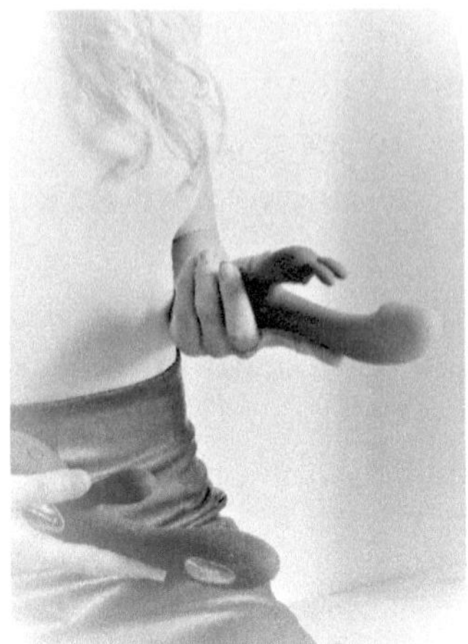

There is a wide variation of toys for adults, among which are:
- Penetration toys: Dildos (from the word Italian "dileto" meaning delight), Dongs, Balls, etc.
- Vibrating toys: for penetration or external use
- Penis rings
- Creams, lubricants, etc.

Incorporating "Sex Toys" into the relationship may require good communication about the couple's preferences, likes and dislikes, so that, in an open and uninhibited way, you two can give each other pleasure.

Explicit Videos:

The use of "explicit adult's video" can be another interesting addition for couples. If you keep an open mind and look at it as mere distraction it can be a positive addition.

Pornography, printed or visual, is the material containing the explicit description or display of sexual organs or activity, intended to stimulate erotic rather than aesthetic or emotional feelings.

Most of this type of meaterial is produced with men in mind, but there can also be found some produced for women.

Likewise, consider that there is also material of extremely poor quality, therefore, try to be selective in your search. Now a days, from the privacy of your home, through the Internet you can buy these and many other sexual related materials.

The most important thing for this type of material to be helpful to the couple, is that both make the decision to expand the discovery in your sexuality.

In an uninhibited way, with trust, with sincere interest, and with doors open for communication, the couple can go on a journey of discovery for fun and pleasure.

You can make it a project that together you two will carry out and go on, be playful and delight each other.

Contraceptive Methods

Sex for the exclusive purpose of procreation is in the past, nowadays, a pregnancy can be planned or avoided.

There are various methods that, according to personal preference, can be chosen. What follows in this chapter is a general overview of common methods that can be available.

Ultimately the decision for the right contraceptive method that the couple choses should be done between them and their Doctor.

Let us remember that for pregnancy to occur sperm produced by the man and the ova produced by the woman, during her ovulation period, will need to bind into one. Then the fertilized egg is deposited and develops within the womb (the uterus).

Contraceptive methods are intended to prevent this natural phenomenon from happening. Ovulation occurs about 14 days before menstruation.

Listing some common contraceptive methods, we have:

1. Abstinence
2. Condom (Condom)
3. Contraceptive Implant (Implanon and Nexplanon)
4. IUD (Intra uterine device like Mirena)

5.   Contraceptive Pill
6.   Injectable Contraceptive (Depo-Provera)
7.   Contraceptive Sponge (Today Sponge)
8.   Vaginal Contraceptive Ring (NuvaRing)
9.   Breastfeeding as a method of contraception
10.   Cervical Layer (FemCap)
11.   Spermicide
12.   Surgical female sterilization
13.   Vasectomy (Surgical male sterilization)
14.   Contraceptive patch (like Ortho Evra)
15.   Coitus Interruptus - "Finish Outside"
16.   The after-sex pill
17.   **Essure** was designed as an implantable **birth control** device that permanently blocked the fallopian tubes in women. The manufacturer of the **Essure** system of birth control removed the device from the U.S. market in January 2019)

ABSTINENCE:

For contraceptive purposes refers to avoiding the penetration of the penis into the vagina. Therefore, not delivering the sperm during ejaculation to meet the ova and avoiding pregnancy.

THE RHYTHM METHOD:

This method is not very secure and assumes that the woman has mostly regular periods, therefore ovulates at a predictable time of the cycle. A simple way to calculate: From the anticipated date when it will start the next menstruation take 20 days off, from that date avoid sex for the next 10 days that they are the ones with the highest risk of pregnancy.

A more detailed calculation: Within the last 6 to 10 periods, **Determine the length of your shortest menstrual cycle.** Subtract 18 from the total number of days in your shortest cycle. This number represents the first fertile day of your cycle. For example, if your shortest cycle is 26 days long, subtract 18 from 26—which equals 8. In this example, the first day of your cycle is the first day of menstrual bleeding and the eighth day of your cycle is the first fertile day. Then, **Determine the length of your longest menstrual cycle.** Subtract 11 from the total number of days in your longest cycle. This number represents the last fertile day of your cycle. For example, if your longest cycle is 32 days long, subtract 11 from 32—which equals 21. In this example, the first day of your cycle is the first day of menstrual bleeding and the 21st day of your cycle is the last fertile day.

PRESERVATIVE:

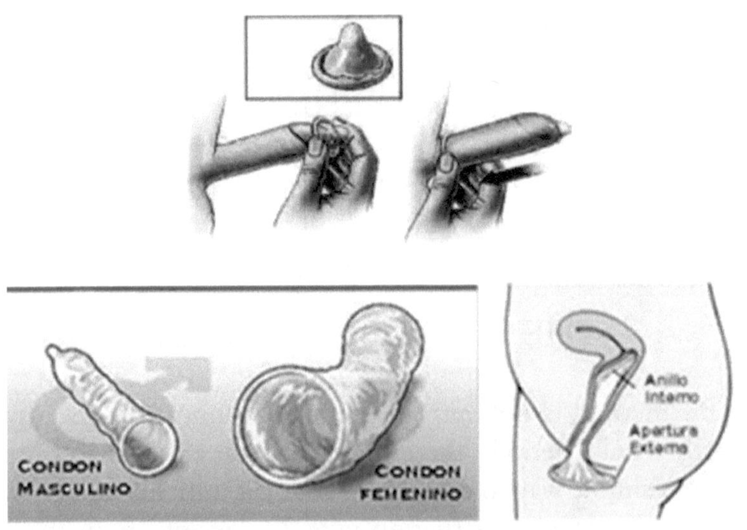

The application of the condom before the sexual act, before penetration, protects against pregnancy and against venereal diseases.

CONTRACEPTIVE IMPLANT:

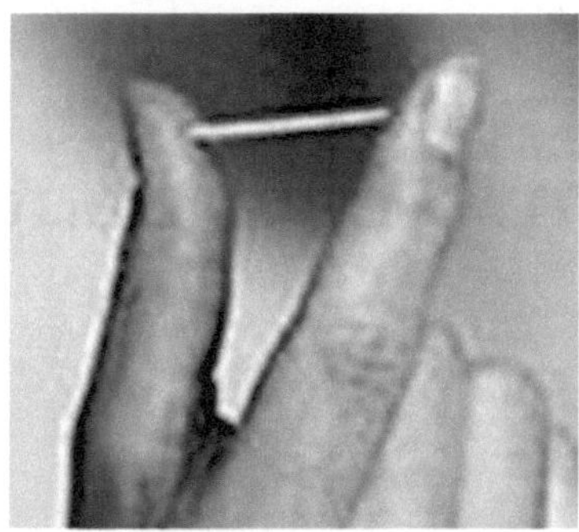

A plastic tube is placed on the arm below the skin, releases a hormone Progestin, and avoid ovulation in addition to forming a thick mucus that avoids sperm enter the uterus. Protects for 3 years.

The INTRAUTERINE DEVICE implant (IUD):

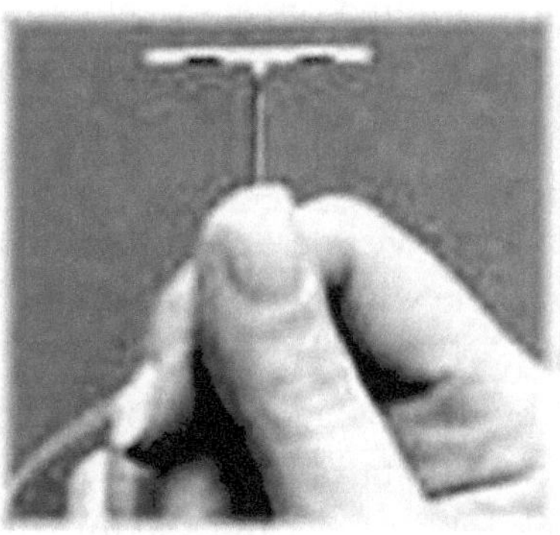

During menstruation, the Gynecologist, in his
office, inserts this device into the uterus. It can be from copper (Paragard-hormone free) that can work up to 10 years. The hormonal (Mirena) can last up to 8 years. They avoid egg release and prevent implantation of the fertilized ovum in the endometrium (inner lining

of the uterus). They could cause irregularity in the menstrual cycle, usually not recommended for people having multiple partners since STD problems could be more serious. Also, it is usually less advisable for nulliparous (women who did not have a previous delivery).

ANTIVCOCEPTIVE PATCH:

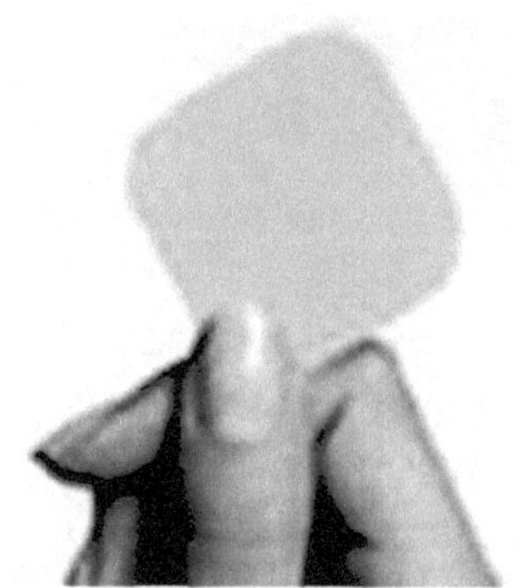

(Ortho-Evra) It is applied once a week, and the fourth week is patch-free. The menstruation starts in the fourth week and proceed to repeat this in a cyclical form. Pros: Easy application and easy to remember once per week. Disadvantages: In some people it may irritate the skin, it may be visible depending on where it is applied, rarely, especially in people who sweat a lot could come off. Like with most hormonal products, rarely, it may have some of the side effects like those produced by the contraceptive pill. Within the first 5 days that the menstrual period starts, apply the patch, then change one new patch every week for 3 weeks and the fourth week no need for a patch, then restart cycle. The way it works is by releasing hormones that prevent ovulation and form a thick mucus that prevents the penetration of sperm to the womb.

THE CONTRACEPTIVE PILL:

This is quite a convenient and pretty effective method. They come in packages of 21 or 28 days, start the first week that menstruation begins and take a pill every day, preferably at the same hour to develop a routine. In packages of 21 days, when finished, wait a week, and start a new package. For those 28 days, start a new package as soon as the used package is finished. Recently the morning day after pill has become available too.

They contain hormones and work by preventing ovulation and producing a thick mucosa that covers the cervix preventing the penetration of sperm to the womb. The BCP (birth control pills) have been associated to abnormal blood clot formation, especially in smokers.

Advantages: Easy to take, one tablet daily, effective in preventing pregnancy if taken correctly, relatively low cost. May help regulate menstrual periods and decrease the amount of blood loss during menstruation.

Disadvantages: Potential side effects including nausea, headache, melasma (spots on the face), menstrual irregularity, small risk of blood clot formation. There is a need to take a tablet daily without forgetting.

INJECTABLE CONTRACEPTIVE:

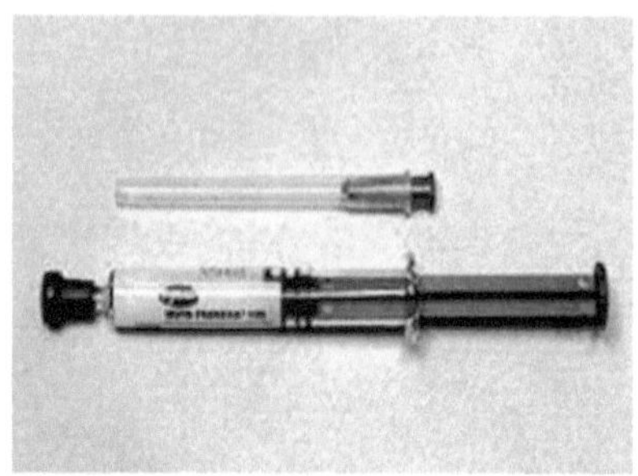

The medicine is injected with vial containing progesterone (DepoProvera)

and can prevent pregnancy for 12 weeks. Works avoiding ovulation and forming a mucus that prevents sperm from entering the matrix.

CONTRACEPTIVE SPONGE:

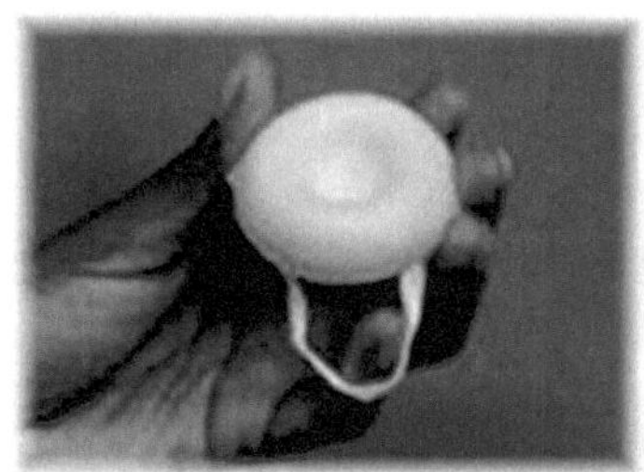

Made of a fluffy plastic material (Today Sponge), need to introduce it deep in the vagina up to 24 hours before having sex, leave it on for 6 hours after the sexual act and remove it in less than a total of 36 hours. Its effectiveness ranges between 70 and 90%. Less efficient in women that were previously pregnant. It works by covering the entrance from the womb to the sperm.

VAGINAL CONTRACEPTIVE RING:

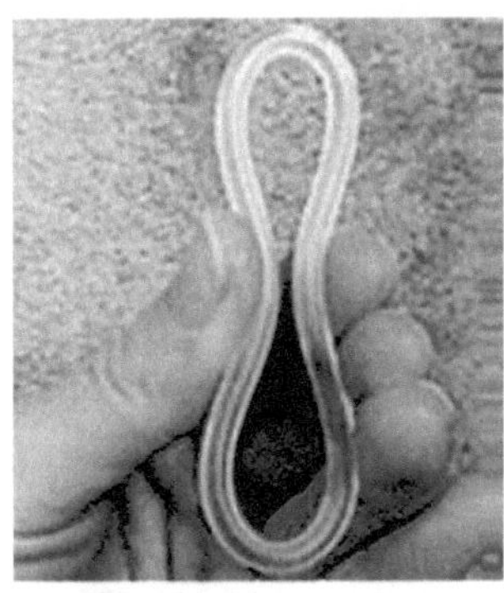 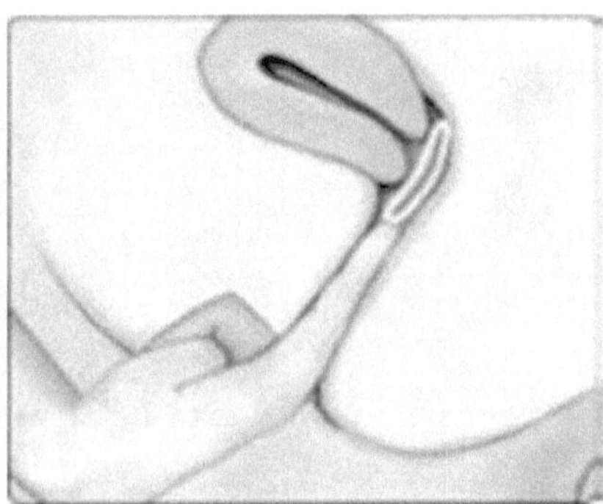

Advantages: Easy to apply, less chance of bleeding between menses.

Disadvantages: Some women they might not like the idea to put a plastic ring in the vagina. Like all hormonal products, it could rarely have some side effects, like those produced by the contraceptive pill. It is inserted into the vagina in the first five days that the menstrual period begins. It needs to stay in place inside the vagina for 3 weeks, then the fourth week (day 22 of having inserted into the vagina) remove it, one week no ring and then restart the same cycle. Effective between 91 and 99%. Releases hormones preventing ovulation and forming a mucus that covers the cervix on admission of the sperm.

BREAST-FEEDING:

During the first 6 months after delivery, that the woman breast-feeds as the exclusive source of feeding for her baby, she likely will not have menstrual periods or ovulate, therefore, will have small chance of getting pregnant. But, for increased safety, it is recommended to use an additional contraceptive method.

CERVICAL COVERTOR (FemCap):

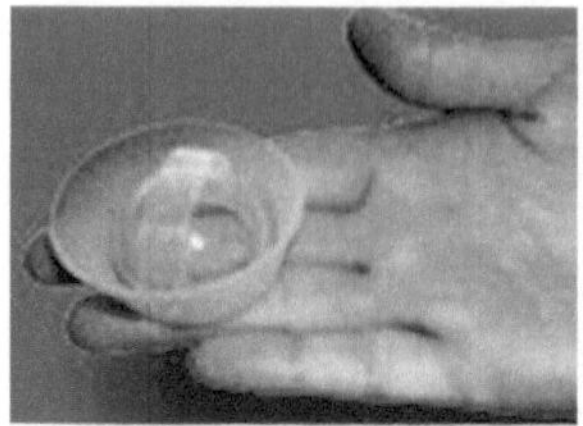

Using a spermicide cream, as lubricant, introduce it deeply in vagina before the sexual act, leave it for 6 hours after the ejaculation. It is efficient only 70 to 86% of the time. It works by producing a barrier to penetration of the sperm into the womb, and the cream spermicide destroys the sperm.

SPERMICIDE:

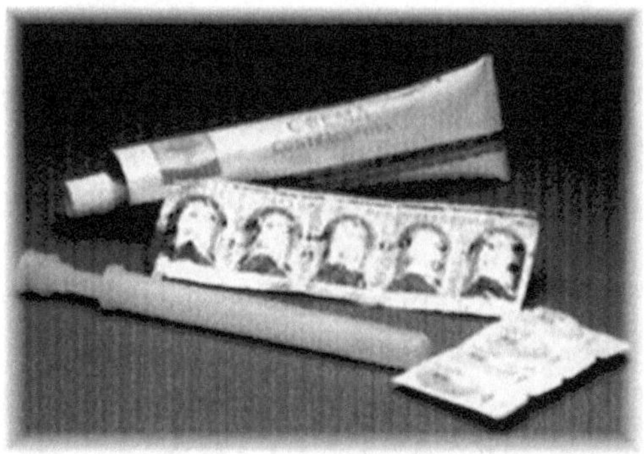

Chemical substances in a cream, gel or vaginal suppository that is introduced in the vagina before penetration, its effect lasts only one hour and need not douche for 6 hours later. Works with chemicals that paralyze the sperm preventing it from progressing to the ovum. They are only efficient 70 to 85% of the times and can cause local irritation.

FEMALE SURGICAL STERILIZATION:

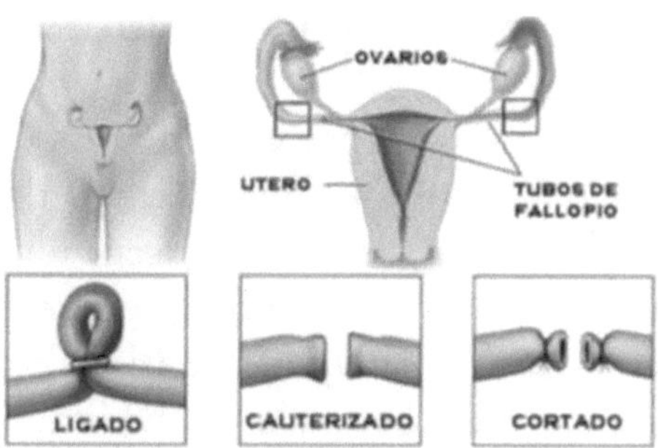

Usually via laparoscopy, through a small incision in the abdominal wall, the fallopian tubes path will be interrupted by ligature, cut, burn, or remove a portion and thus avoid communication between the ovum and the spermatozoa. It is a permanent method, very safe but invasive and expensive.

VASECTOMY:

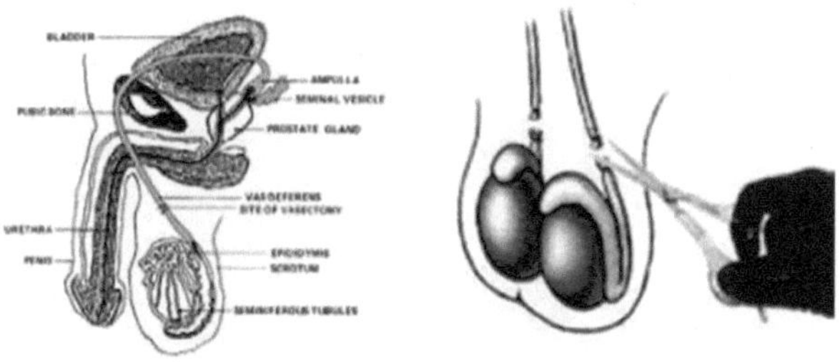

Surgical procedure performed in the Urologist's office, where the Doctor will proceed to cut the tube (Vas deferens) that carries the sperm into the urinary tract during ejaculation. Therefore, the ejaculation will no longer have spermatozoids, and will no longer be able to get his lady pregnant. The man should wait about 3 months after procedure then have his ejaculation be checked to make sure there is no viable sperm before being sure that the procedure worked. In the mean while another additional contraceptive method should be used to prevent pregnancy. It is considered a safe and efficient permanent procedure.

There are many ways to prevent pregnancy, and you should consult with your doctor to find our which is the most appropriate birth control method in your case. Except for the condom, the other contraceptive methods do not offer protection against venereal diseases. I reiterate that ultimately the decision in choosing the best contraceptive method must be made by the individual in conjunction with his/her doctor.

Venereal Diseases

Those diseases that are transmitted through sexual contact are known as Venereal diseases.(STD,STI)

This section does not pretend to give neither diagnosis nor treatment, just some basic information to alert the person as to when might be a good idea to check with the doctor.

After unprotected sex (no condom), the symptoms that suggest that the person could have an infection sexually transmittable include:

- Burning when urinating
- Itching, or irritation of the genitals
- Bad smell in your genital area.
- Abnormal redness of your genitals.
- Pain when having sex.
- Unusual discharge either from the vagina or penis, especially when it is thick, whitish, or yellowish.
- Appearance of sores, ulcers, bumps on the skin and / or mucosa of the vagina, penis, or on the surrounding areas.
- Pain in the pelvic region.

Symptoms could be of sudden or gradual onset, sometimes they could even be accompanied by fever, chills, nausea, vomiting, prostration, and general discomfort.

On the other hand, the lack of symptoms does not ensure that the individual does not have an infection. The condition known as "Asymptomatic carrier" is when the person has the infection and, can transmit the illness but does not have any discomfort.

This last point is quite important especially when one has symptoms and is diagnosed by the doctor to have a venereal disease, even if the partner has no discomfort, equally, BOTH should be treated to avoid re-infection.

Among the communicable sexually diseases that have treatment and cure are: Gonorrhea, Syphilis, Chlamydia, Trichomonas.

Among those STD's that have no cure are: Genital Herpes, Viral Hepatitis C or B, and the Immunodeficiency Virus (HIV). For these conditions there may be treatment that mitigates the condition or controls the symptoms.

There are other conditions that require local treatment such as genital warts and condylomas (with local chemicals, freezing therapy, locally burning the lesion, etc.).

HPV is one of the most common STI's affecting about 42 million Americans.

Typically harmless (most clear the virus on their own without complications) the virus can lead to cervical and oropharyngeal cancers in some cases.

It is also worth mentioning that not all genital diseases are sexually transmissible, for example, Vaginal Candidiasis caused by Candida Albicans, and Vaginosis caused by Gardnerella Vaginalis are not sexually transmitted.

If you are suspecting a genital infection, check with your doctor, as failure to do so could progress and produce complications including Sterility (inability to become pregnant), Sepsis (infection in the blood), or even death.

It should be noted that monogamy (relationship exclusive between two people) makes the acquisition of a venereal infection improbable.

XXIII

Sexual Pathologies

Sexual dysfunctions are a lot more common than most people imagine.

According to a magazine of the American Medical Association, in an interview with people between 18 to 59 years, it was observed that the sexual dysfunction was up to 43% in women and 31% in men. It was also seen, that, most of these cases, were treatable.

Sexual dysfunction is an important public health concern, and emotional problems are frequently associated to these problems.

Among the sex problems, most frequently reported, in men are: Erectile dysfunction, Premature ejaculation, and lack of interest.

Among women the most frequently reported are: Lack of sexual appetite, problems with stimulation, difficulties reaching an orgasm and painful conditions during the sexual act.

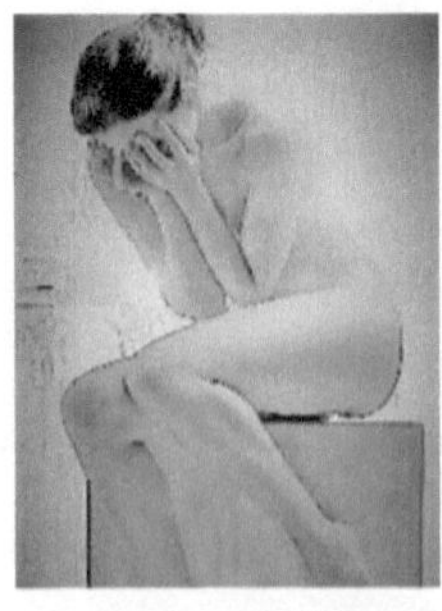

Sexual Impotence: (Erectile Dysfunction) - ED

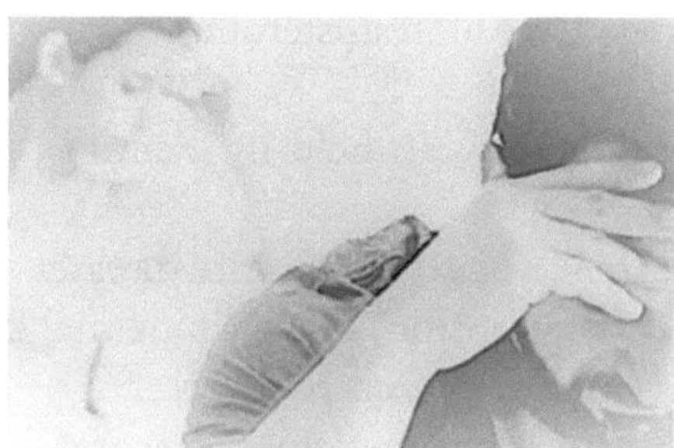

The difficulty or impossibility of having or maintaining a good erection of the penis, so that it allows intercourse, is known as Erectile Dysfunction.

It can be transitory or permanent, it can occur at any age, but it is more frequent in advanced adult age.

For a proper erection to occur several are the factors that must be working adequately, and in coordination. Between these factors we have:

▶ The psychological aspect: Which is of most importance. As an example, the feelings of rejection, anxiety, and depression can prevent an erection.

▶ The nervous system: It is the one that regulates the sensation, contraction and relaxation of muscles and blood vessels. Dysfunction of this system, as in the case of Diabetes Mellitus, can cause ED.

▶ The circulatory system: It is responsible of distributing the blood throughout the organism. For the erection to occur the corpora cavernosa of the penis must get filled of blood, when the circulation is affected, the erection is not good.

▶ The hormonal system: The production of the male hormone Testosterone, which occurs primarily in the testicles, has a determinant influence in both the sexual desire and the sexual potency, and when this system is not working properly, the sexual function is negatively affected. A simple blood test can determine the level of Testosterone.

The following factors can help us identify the probable cause or ED:

- The existence of concomitants diseases such as Diabetes, arterial Hypertension, Hyperlipidemia, etc. Suggest a nervous or vascular system problem.
- There are multiple medicines, that as a side effect, can produce ED, consult your doctor.
- When there is a regular erection on awaking in the morning, but there is no erection when the person wants to have intercourse can suggest a psychological problem.

In addition to identifying the cause of the ED and managing this problem (with your Doctor), there are, at present time, multiple methods to treat Erectile Dysfunction. There are oral medicines that can help increase blood flow towards the genitals thus helping the erection. (Example: Viagra, Levitra, Cialis, generics, etc.). There are injectable intramuscular medicines, and others that are inserted into the penis, etc. When necessary, there are surgical procedures and implants.

When sexual impotence is not transient, it is advisable to consult with your doctor to receive adequate treatment. It may be needed to search for the underlying problem and then proceed to treat it.

Premature Ejaculation: (PE)

Orgasm and emission of semen occurring just before or shortly after beginning sexual intercourse, earlier than him or his partner would prefer.

Premature Ejaculation can affect to both in the relationship: for the man the enjoyment was very brief and for the woman she barely began to feel stimulated and "the show is over".

This condition can be caused by various factors, one of the most important being the anxiety factor. There are medicines that have proven to improve this problem, check with your doctor.

Frequently can be a combination of ED and PE. Subconsciously he finishes quickly anticipating the erection will go down before ejaculating.

Here some helpful tips to "last longer":

→ When the man feels that the stimulus is advancing and is about to reach the "point of no return", that is before the impending sense of desire to ejaculate, at that time the man can distract his mind with something non-sexual, he can interrupt sexual stimulation, avoid friction, discontinue penetration, and press on the perineum (place between the anus and the base of the penis) for a brief moment to then resume sexual activity. Also pressing under the head of the penis can help.

→ There is an exercise that many help men with premature ejaculation. He can, either alone or with the help of his partner, masturbate to get an erection but avoid ejaculation by interrupting the friction every time he is close to ejaculation. Repeat this maneuver as many times as possible.

→ OTC St. John Wort has shown to help.

→ There are also medications that his Doctor can prescribe.

Anorgasmia:

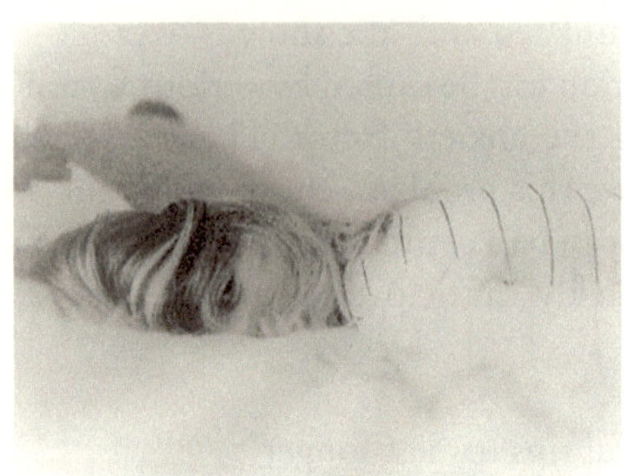

It refers to the difficulty, and sometimes to the impossibility, of being able to reach an orgasm, and it may be due to multiple causes. Orgasm is a complex reaction to various physical, emotional, and psychological factors. Difficulties in any of these areas can affect the ability to orgasm.

→ **Physical causes** A wide range of illnesses, physical changes and medications can interfere with orgasm:

Diseases: Serious illnesses, such as Major Depression, multiple sclerosis, and Parkinson's disease, are often associated with difficulty achieving an orgasm.

Gynecological issues: Infections can be associated to painful intercourse. Gynecologic surgeries, such as hysterectomy or cancer surgeries, can affect orgasm.

Medications: Many over the counter and prescription medications can negatively affect orgasm, including blood pressure medications, antipsychotic drugs, antihistamines, and antidepressants (SSRIs).

Alcohol and smoking: Too much alcohol can hamper your ability to climax. Smoking can limit blood flow to your sexual organs.

Aging: As you age, normal changes in your anatomy, hormones, neurological system, and circulatory system can affect your sexuality. Lowering estrogen levels as women transition into menopause and menopausal symptoms, such as night sweats and mood changes, can have an impact on sexuality.

→ **Psychological causes:**
Many psychological factors can play a role in your ability to orgasm, including Mental health problems, such as anxiety or low self-esteem, Poor body image, Stress and financial pressures, Cultural and religious beliefs, Bashfulness, Guilt about enjoying sex, Past sexual or emotional abuse.

Relationship issues

Non-sexual problems can affect sexual relationship. Issues such as Lack of connection with your partner, Unresolved conflicts, Poor communication of sexual needs and preferences, Infidelity or breach of trust, Violence, Disrespect, etc.

Sex education can be useful, improving interpersonal relationships with your partner. Other measures, depending on the case could include: Hormone replacement administered by your physician (when determined hormonal deficiency is present, but not so for all cases), local application to the clitoris of creams that facilitate blood flow (Viacreme), the use of Eros Therapy (prescription device that sucks the clitoris increasing the sensitivity of their genitals), etc. Check with your doctor or a Sex Therapist.

Vaginism:

The involuntary spasmodic contraction of the muscles at the entrance to the vagina is known as Vaginismus. This condition can interfere and even prevent penetration and consequent sexual intercourse. Mainly it is due to psychological causes.

<u>Dispareunia:</u>

Pain during sexual intercourse is often due to physical causes such as vaginal infections, lack of adequate lubrication, rough sex, local trauma, or other conditions. Sometimes they can be due to psychological conditions or negative feelings about a partner.

The man can also suffer from this condition.

If you suffer from this condition you should consult with your doctor.

XXIV

Suggestions about what a partner may like to have done to him or Her

The difference between women and men is evident in many respects.

To begin with, the development of their sexual organs is different. The male genitalia is external and easily accessible, while female genitalia is "more hidden". Men easily learn that touch leads to pleasant sensations, the visual stimulus is also more marked in men. In women the emotional factor, and the imagination play a more important role in their ability to enjoy intimacy.

The following presentation is based in an informal survey of couples of different ages and educational levels, who mentioned about their sexual likings and cravings, and made suggestions that they would like to have done to them or them do to their mates.

This chapter can serve to reinforce what you are already practicing or to discover some suggestions that you may choose to apply with your partner.

It should be noted that the information presented below, the result of the contribution of many couples, should be seen as simply a list of suggestions that may or may not apply to your situation.

WHAT SOME WOMEN SAID THEY WOULD LIKE:

- ▶ That he surprises me with giving me a massage under the light of an aromatic candle, and with relaxing music.
- ▶ That he buys for me "sexy" underwear that he himself chose it.
- ▶ That he notices when I change my appearance, or I dress in a special different way, and that he also likes and approves it.
- ▶ That he gives me perfumes with a pleasant aroma for him.

▶ That he sends me flowers for no special reason, with a suggestive message, and make me feel that he is always thinking in me.

▶ That in advance, he calls me to tell me not to cook because we are going out to eat, or that he will prepare dinner at home.

▶ That he frequently tells me nice things about what he likes about me, compliments such as how soft my skin is, the sweet and tender look I have, the color of my eyes, etc.

▶ That he would allow more space for spontaneity.

▶ That he voices some sweet or affectionate words, and subtle noises of pleasure during our sexual intimacy.

▶ That he shows his interest in spending time with me and doing things that I also like.

▶ That he would feel that "giving pleasure to your partner gives also pleasure to oneself".

▶ That he would be more considerate and pay more attention to the details.

▶ That he continues to make me feel "protected" in his arms and in his presence.

▶ That he makes me feel that I can count on him.

▶ That he would take my opinions into account, and to make me participate also in the important things that happen in his life.

▶ That he makes me feel "pampered."

▶ That he had displays of affection not only in private, but in all places, and no matter who is present.

▶ That he has good hygiene, good breath and often uses perfume with manly aroma.

▶ That he would not bring work problems to home, and that he stayed in a good mood.

OF SEXUAL CONNOTATION- Some ladies said: "I would like…"

- For him to continue kissing me passionately like at the beginning.
- For him tell me about what he likes me to do to him, the parts of his body that he likes to be kissed, the way he likes me to do it, so that I know it, and I can please him better.
- That, when we make love, he takes me firmly and makes me feel like I belong to him.
- For him to give me oral sex.
- For him to suck me over and around my clitoris, and simultaneously fiddles with the tip of his tongue on the tip of it.
- For him to lick me with his full tongue, from the bottom to top, repeatedly, on my vulva, and from time to time, inserts his tongue into my vagina.
- For him to be soft, delicate, and tender at the beginning of his caresses directed to my whole body.
- For him to touch me gently on my head and the back of my neck, while I am giving him oral sex.
- For him to be mischievous, naughty and playfully and touch me in my "private" areas in public places, but without anyone else noticing.

- For him to take me tightly in his arms, full of passion, so that I can "abandon myself", and feel that I am at the mercy of my partner.
- And some ladies also said:
- When we are making love, looking at each other, I like for him, with his hands, to press on my buttocks firmly against his body.
- I like that he takes the initiative and I follow the rhythm that he leads us.
- I like to get into a crawling position and have him penetrate me from behind.
- I like that when I am, facing down, on my stomach and he is on top of me, penetrating me from behind, he places his hand forward, exerting pressure on my vulva.
- I would like him to feel free to take me as he wants, when he wants, and for me to do the same.
- I like him to kiss me and gently suck on my neck at the same time as he penetrates me from behind.
- I like that, at the same time he is massaging my back, he inserts his penis into my vagina and moves rhythmically.

WHAT MEN LIKE:

GENERALITIES- What men said: "I would like…"

- ▶ For her to flirt with me often.
- ▶ That she dresses up and gets sexy for me.
- ▶ That she keeps me present in her mind and heart all the time.
- ▶ That she takes good care of her personal hygiene and, has a pleasant feminine aroma.
- ▶ That she waits for me with open arms, a sweet sincere smile, lots of kisses, and the food ready, when I return from work.
- ▶ That, without being asked, she prepares the things that I like.
- ▶ That the children are well cared for, the house in order, and the clothes clean and organized.

▶ That she has a formal and demure attitude with everyone, but that with me she "uncovers" and gets adventurous and daring.

▶ That she shows me that she appreciates what I do for the family and, that she tells me that she is proud of me.

▶ That she does not get upset if I call on her a mistake, or something that I would like her to do differently, but to the contrary, that she shows interest in what I pointed out and corrects it in a pleasant way.

▶ That she does not insult me or express herself in a rude or derogatory manner towards me.

▶ That she, at her own initiative, surprises me with a massage.

▶ That she would never, in a negative way, compare me with others, even worse with some of her "ex".

▶ That she does not disrespect me, specially, in public.

▶ That she would stop criticizing and fighting with me all the time.

▶ For her not to be jealous, even worse when it is the of product of her imagination.

▶ That she caresses me, hugs, and kisses me as often as possible.

▶ That she would know how to value what she receives and stop wanting everything that others have.

▶ That she be considered in her expenses and lives according to our own real economic situation.

▶ That she keeps our intimate life private just between the two of us.

▶ That she does not get influenced by her friends' opinions, and that she has her own opinion and set of values.

Of Sexual Connotation:

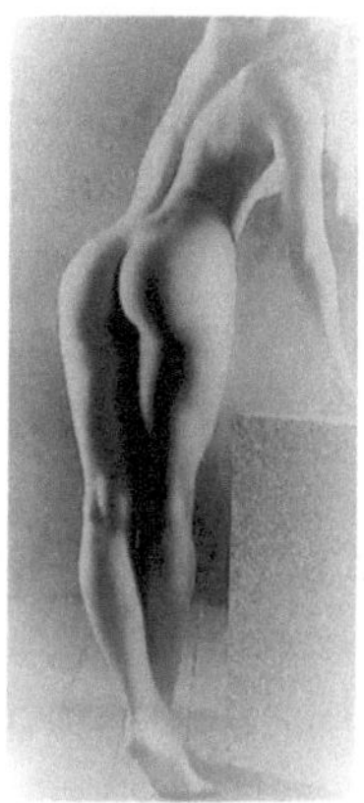

- I would like her, at her own initiative, to dress sexy and provoke me.
- I like that she gives me oral sex frequently.
- I would like her to frequently have a seductive attitude directed only towards me.
- That, at least, from time to time, she would surprise me and take the initiative in our "love nest".
- I would like to hear her gasping with pleasure, as well as feel her contorting her body, between my arms, full of joy and pleasure. To let her emotions wide open and loud during our intimacy.
- I like to see that she prepares, in advance, our evening of love, dressing up with intimate and sexy clothes as well as decorating our bedroom for the occasion.
- I would like her to get playful and "attack" me with caresses and kisses, provoking me into love making.
- I would like to receive massage from her frequently, and then continue to sexual intimacy.

- I would like for her not to interrupt my sexual advances, to the contrary, to feed into them even more, participating and enjoying actively.
- I would like that, when I am tired, she masturbates me and gives me oral sex until I climax.
- I would like for her, from time to time, to stimulate me in my G-spot (The Prostate).
- I like for her to insert my penis into her mouth as deeply as possible.
- I would like for her to, at the same time she sucks my penis, she rubs her tongue against it.
- I would like for her to be docile, pleasing and accommodating to my sexual advances and to letting our imagination free to seek pleasuring each other.
- I would like her not to stay stiff, motionless as a piece of furniture, and to actively participate when we make love.
- I like that if I ever finish earlier, that she does not complain.
- I would like for her not to get scandalized or offended when suggesting and making all imaginable delights in our privacy.
- I would like her, at least, occasionally, to ask me to make love, and to let me know that she wants me, that she desires me.
- I would like her to get playful and have fun with any new experimentation we do in bed.
- I like her to suck on all my fingers.
- I like that she plays with her tongue on my neck, my back, between my legs, and all over my body.
- I would like her to make love to me in all possible places, and at all possible times.
- I would like her to massage me, not only with her hands, but also with her legs, buttocks, breasts and to slide her hair over my body.

- I would like for her to show me with actions what she says to me with words, loving me passionately and giving me pleasure frequently.
- I would like for her to feel and show me that "making love" is a manifestation of love, and that she looks forward to our love making, every day and at every possible moment.

XXV

Final Comments

The great importance of sexuality in human beings and in the couple is clearly established. Likewise, it has been clearly established that, to be able to give stability to the relationship, it is indispensable the active and positive participation of both in the couple. It is a two-way street; you both give and receive.

It is essential that both of you feed a positive and proactive attitude into the relationship. Give fuel to the fire of passion, have a nonjudgmental attitude with uninhibited dedication, perseverance, attention, strength, and a lot of love.

Rejection kills desire, passion, and can destroy the relationship. Likewise, sex or the lack of it should never be used as a revenge weapon.

Effective communication has a most important and indispensable role. As long as there is good communication, there will be hope. When communication is lacking it will be, not only difficult, but unlikely to maintain the union in the couple.

The man especially values that his partner demonstrates to him that she respects, appreciates, and wants him with passion. To reiterate, keep in mind that, for men APPRECIATION, RESPECT and being DESIRED are especially important.

On the other hand, women especially value that her partner demonstrates to her that he loves her, protects her, and admires her.

For her ADMIRATION, PROTECTION and ROMANTICISM with love are of most importance.

When these conditions are present, there will be a solid base so that, in an environment of mutual trust, both can give themselves completely to each other and "Make love with love".

This book has been written for the couple, and takes for granted that, if both are together as a couple, it is because there was that day when they mutually conquered each other and gave themselves to each other with love.

Most relationships when they begin have fire, passion, gallantry, tenderness, mystery, and frequent manifestations of love.

To preserve all these beautiful things and grow even more in their love giving, both of you should continue to conquer each other continuously.

"In the relationship, each one is responsible for
its own sexual satisfaction, its own emotional
stability, and especially, each one is responsible
for their half in the relationship".

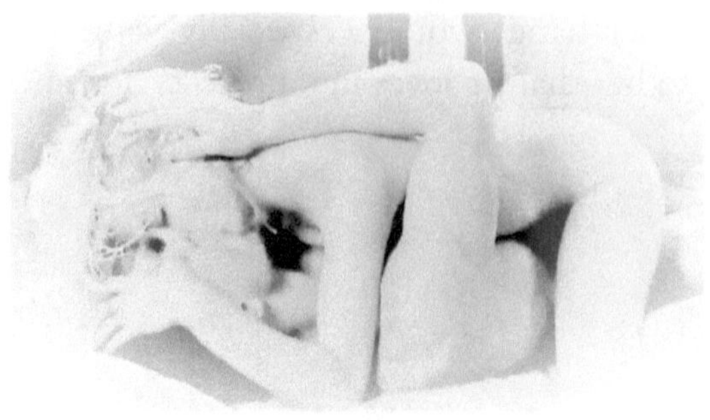

In human relationships, when it comes to intimacy, there is no "formula" or "recipe" that works for everyone. Each human being is a unique and an individual entity (a being with distinct and independent existence).

Therefore, this book should be taken as a contribution of useful information, full of suggestions aimed at helping the couple. Ultimately, each couple will see what works for them and what does not.

This book is not intended to diagnose or treat any condition. It is not intended to replace the intervention of medical attention, or the visit to a sex therapist (when necessary), it is only intended to be a useful guide about important concepts in sexuality and relationship for the couple.

In life there are no guarantees, and people can only do their best to make things go well… keep going on, feeding your love, and moving forward with great enthusiasm, and dedication.

Especially keep doing nice things for each other, like when you started the relationship, and you conquered each other. Be happy and enjoy fully your love with fire and passion.

—The author.

About the Author

Leonnardo Andre (Pseudonym) is a Medical Doctor, with more than 30 years of experience, currently working in private practice. He believes that a human being is an integral entity: Mind, body, and spirit.

"Patients look for relief of their physical illnesses, but specially they look to fulfill their emotional needs, they search to receive recognition from those people that are important in their lives, especially validation by their mates."

After a few years in practice, I saw the need to offer my patients a source of reliable information that could help them in their relationships. A guide easy to comprehend that could help develop a better understanding about sexuality in their lives.

To my surprise I could not find a book that looked at Sexuality in a more wholesome way. I was looking for a book with simple language that contained correct, scientific based information, and especially one that would give to "<u>love</u>" the importance as the main engine to promote and give meaningful value to sexuality in their lives.